CUTTING THROUGH THE HYPE

A Taxpayer's Guide To School Reforms

JANE L. DAVID AND LARRY CUBAN

EDUCATION WEEK PRESS

ISBN 0-9674795-5-X

To order copies of this book,
Telephone: (800) 788-5692
Fax: (815) 734-5864
Online: http://edweek.k-online.biz
Or write: Education Week Press
P.O. Box 554, Mt. Morris, IL 61054

Visit us on the Web at edweek.org.

Also From Education Week Press:

To my remarkable mother, Ruth, and to my soul mate, David,
for their unwavering love and support. —JLD

To Barbara for her love, heartfelt wisdom,
and unshakable strength. —LC

Contents

Preface

Our collaboration on this book stems from a 40-year friendship that began in August 1966 at Cardozo High School in Washington, D.C.

In 1963, Larry left a high school teaching job in a Cleveland ghetto to become a master teacher in history for the Cardozo Project in Urban Teaching—a school-based university program training returned Peace Corps volunteers and recent college graduates to become teachers. In 1965, he became director of the program. And, in late August 1966, Larry was desperate. School was to start in less than two weeks, and he had just learned that the federal grant supporting the Cardozo Project would cover the hiring of two math interns. He had found one, but had to have a second to justify a math program.

Jane, meanwhile, had just finished college in Oklahoma, one course shy of a math major. Heading east to find interesting work, she was about to give up after reading all the ads for secretaries and gal Fridays in New York and Boston. Having sworn off teaching and math, coming from a family of teachers, Jane ended up housesitting for friends in Washington when the phone rang. A friend of the homeowners was calling everyone she knew trying to find an aspiring math teacher for her friend Larry Cuban.

Larry interviewed Jane the next day and, with some reluctance due to her lack of enthusiasm about teaching, hired her on the spot. To the surprise of both, Jane loved teaching, in spite of the fact that it was by far the most difficult job she would ever hold. After several years, Jane left for graduate school at Harvard University to study education research and policy while Larry stayed on as a teacher in the District of Columbia and later moved to the central office to administer the district's staff development program.

After a brief stint in the federal government, Jane moved to Palo Alto, Calif., to work at a think tank and then on her own as an independent researcher and consultant, studying efforts to reform schools for poor and minority students. In 1981, Larry moved to Palo Alto to take a faculty position at Stanford University, after serving as the superintendent of the Arlington, Va., Public Schools for seven years.

Reuniting on the West Coast, we have met monthly for lunch for more than 20 years. Many of the ideas in this book were topics of discussion and debate over those many lunches together.

For both of us, teaching in an all-black inner-city school in the midst of the civil rights movement was a formative experience. Committed to the belief that public schools could be good schools for all students, we struggled with the ideals of the reform we were part of against the reality and tough questions we faced daily: How to teach algebra to students who struggled with simple arithmetic? How to teach history to students who could barely read and had never left their immediate neighborhood? How to get help for students in dire need of housing or medical attention? How to convince parents we were calling to report *good* news? Many of our assumptions were naive—we admit we were innocent about the power of institutional patterns to shape behavior and the long-term effects of poverty—just as many reformers' expectations are naive today.

To this day, we struggle with many of the same issues we had to face at Cardozo High School. We maintain a passionate commitment to the public school system—the backbone of an informed electorate and essential in a democratic society. We also maintain a fervent belief that reform is not only possible but also obligatory, and that too many public schools in urban and rural America are shameful. In fact, it is this passion that causes us to raise questions about current reform policies, their implementation, and school practice.

We also believe that our joint, rich experiences as teacher, administrator, researcher, evaluator, and historian have taught us a great deal about the promise and perils of school reform that will be valuable to district, state, and federal policymakers, and to practitioners, parents, and concerned citizens—taxpayers all—who, like us, want to make schools better for all children.

Introduction

In this book, we spell out the assumptions underlying reforms that promise better teaching and learning, more effective schools, and more efficient school systems. Our goal is to offer balanced appraisals and to reflect on hard-earned lessons.

Each year, more and more well-intentioned reforms promise to make our schools better. From vouchers to small schools, from high standards and high-stakes testing to merit pay, from school-based management to wireless laptops for every student—the waves of school reforms to make sense of, vote on, and pay for keep coming, and their promises only grow. The momentum continues because Americans believe education is important, and what's important to the public is important to elected officials.

Political leaders capitalize on the public's concern about their schools, often overstating problems to mobilize support for their solutions, while underestimating what teachers and principals have to do to make them work. Reform advocates and, increasingly, corporate leaders with the ear of policymakers, shape school reforms based on some combination of ideology, best guesses, and hope. Seldom are those who must carry out the reforms—principals and teachers—involved in their design.

Meanwhile, researchers and educators have learned many important lessons from decades of ineffective reforms and their unintended side effects. Classroom teachers in particular have accumulated wisdom from trying to implement reforms designed by others. But those who propose reforms virtually never incorporate these important lessons into their mandates for improving schools.

The result is a growing chasm between policymakers' claims and the chance that the reforms will deliver what's promised. What's worse, even as their taxes underwrite new policies, voters in local, state, and national elections have no way to see beyond the hype. Nowhere can interested citizens—or even those who make policy—learn if a proposed reform has any chance of success or what it would take for that to happen. This book aims to fill that void.

Accumulated knowledge and wisdom are unlikely ever to be the driving force behind enacted reforms. But these days, politics too often plays a decisive role. A case in point, as reported by *The New York Times*: In 2004, New York City's mayor, elected by voters to take control of a failing school system, chose a Panel of Educational Inquiry and a new chancellor. The chancellor, in turn, proposed a policy that would force 3rd graders to repeat the grade if they scored too low on the citywide reading and math tests. When a majority of the panel objected, the mayor intervened, fired his representatives on the panel, and appointed new members who voted for the chancellor's recommendation. In this case, naked political muscle trumped evidence.

Politics, however, can be tempered by information and understanding.

Kindergartens, the comprehensive high school, vocational education, and Advanced Placement, for example, were all once proposed by broad-based political coalitions seeking school improvement. In each case, mixtures of ideologies, eye-catching slogans, occasional evidence, and fervent hopes carried the day.

In the past few decades, school reform has been the subject of more systematic study and documentation. Both researchers and practitioners paint similar pictures of the ebb and flow of reforms, what it takes to make them work, and why so many fail. Based on these sources and our own decades of working in and studying individual schools and districts, we set out to analyze many of the reforms that are prominent today. In this book, we spell out the assumptions underlying reforms that promise better teaching and learning, more effective schools, and more efficient school systems. We look at how well the reforms have worked and at what it would take for them to be more successful. Our goal is not to champion particular reforms, but instead to offer balanced appraisals and reflect on hard-learned lessons.

Our intended audience encompasses many classes of citizens, including: policymakers, from local school board members to those in state and federal offices; politicians and business leaders; advocates; educators; parents; union leaders; and researchers in universities and think tanks; as well as other informed citizens. In this book, we collapse these many roles into three somewhat overlapping groups: policymakers, educators, and citizens. Policymakers include those who set

policy and those who promote a particular reform. Educators include teachers and administrators, as well as those who work with and study them. Parents, individual advocates, and other concerned citizens are grouped together as citizens.

The more that policymakers, citizens, and educators understand what reforms can and cannot accomplish, the more they can make sense of the rhetoric that surrounds them. The more policymakers can separate rhetoric from reality and the more they understand about how schools really work, the more constructive their reform policies will be. The more that citizens and educators can make sense of reforms, the more they can participate in the political process that defines problems and propose policy solutions.

Just as media savvy is important in judging advertising hype, reform savvy is important in sorting out the kernel of truth in claims about reforms. And most reforms do have such a kernel. Wiring schools and installing computers, for example, has become popular with policymakers over the past decade. The kernel of truth is that these technologies do in fact have great potential for teaching and learning. Yet putting information technology in classrooms and labs has not translated into frequent or imaginative use.

Many of the traps that reforms encounter are predictable. Others result from ignorance of the resources needed or unwillingness to invest enough to pull them off. No reform is a panacea, yet most of them are sold as if they are. In short, citizens, policymakers, and educators need to be wary of excessive promises, slick packaging, and flawed assumptions.

In this book, we scrutinize claims and jargon while attempting to get to the heart of three crucial questions: Does a reform make sense? Can the reform actually work in classrooms? Are the conditions for success in place? We chose to analyze reforms that have become part of the national discussion and are intended, directly or indirectly, to improve classroom teaching and student learning. For example, a state mandate for a high school graduation test or a district policy to expand the number of charter schools both ultimately aim to improve classroom practice.

The seeds of such reforms may have been planted by the White House, governors, state legislatures, mayors, foundations, unions, think tanks, corporate leaders, local school boards, or a range of others. All of the players try to extend their influence as ideas are reshaped into federal, state, or local policies.

Some reform ideas are new. Many have appeared before, vanished, and were later resurrected. They are often pursued with a vengeance—witness the federal No Child Left Behind legislation with its reliance on tests and accountability—with varying degrees of understanding, support, or disdain from those who work in classrooms daily.

We offer the diagram on the following page for those unfamiliar with the structure of America's decentralized tax-supported education system and the many influences that shape the reform-minded policies spilling forth from federal, state, and district offices. Oversimplified, of course, the diagram's purpose is to show the multilayered system of public schooling and the many players—elected and self-appointed—who introduce reform ideas that eventually become the policies that determine what schools must do. This policy-to-practice diagram also shows the variety of influences and the demands placed upon elected officials to respond to school problems.

Policymakers at each level are the ones who have the authority and resources to take reform ideas and convert them into policies. Although policymakers have worthy aims for public education, they, like most of us, see the world from where they stand. They work in elected and appointed posts where they are constantly beset by individuals and groups seeking to influence their decisions. The arrows outside the box depict some of the many players representing varied interests (e.g., PTAs, unions, chambers of commerce, religious, ethnic and racial groups, CEOs) who lobby policymakers at all levels of the system, frequently and intensely. These interest groups each seek either to initiate new or reshape existing school policies to benefit children— from their respective points of view.

Federal, state, and local policymakers live in a world full of real and imagined crises often triggered by media accounts. Working in highly visible, conflict-ridden settings, policymakers typically listen to many voices and then latch onto what sounds like a good idea. They seldom have time to check out whether evidence supports their decision or whether, indeed, their idea will work when it is fleshed out and

Readers need to consider three crucial questions before signing on for any big-picture changes:

Does a reform make sense?

Can the reform actually work in classrooms?

Are the conditions for success in place?

The Many Influences on Reform: From Policy to Practice

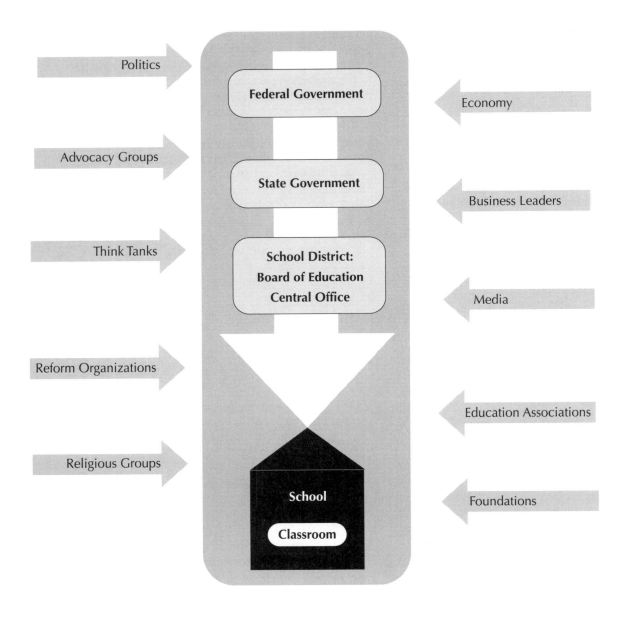

sent along to teachers. Almost none have ever taught, run a school, or superintended a district. They are far removed from the classrooms where they expect their policies to make a difference.

Making the trip from policy to classroom practice is not easy. The journey is like the childhood game where you whisper something to one person who repeats the message to the next person and so on down the line. Typically, the initial message is vastly different from the one the last person hears.

The same distortions occur as policies pass through layers of government and bureaucracy before reaching school principals and classroom teachers. One thing to remember in tracking the progression from policy to practice is that a reform message sent by the White House, governor, state legislature, or school board may not be the one received by teachers.

In our decades of experience and research in this policy-to-practice world we have seen teachers and principals negotiate daily the twists and turns of school and classroom routines. We have participated in, watched, and researched reform policies aimed at improving what happens in classrooms. The reforms inevitably reflect the varied aims of policymakers seeking improvements in student learning by targeting changes in state systems of education, how schools are organized and governed, or, more directly, what is taught and how. Accordingly, we have grouped the reforms that follow into three sections that reflect these different levels: Reforming the system, reforming how

schools are organized, and reforming teaching and learning. Each chapter describes where a particular reform idea originated, the problem it is intended to solve, what we know about its effectiveness, and what it takes to make it work.

We hope that readers will come to better understand which reforms are worth investing in and which ones should be passed up. Ultimately, our intention is for readers to finish this book with a better grasp of what's realistic to expect of highly touted reforms, what trade-offs need to be considered, and what can be done to increase the likelihood that reforms will succeed.

Our goal is for readers to finish this book with a better grasp of what's realistic to expect of highly touted reforms, what trade-offs need to be considered, and what can be done to increase the likelihood that a reform will succeed.

Reforming the System

I n the United States, K-12 public education relies upon a multilayered system in which states hold primary authority and responsibility for setting up and running their own public schools. Beyond that, the federal government contributes a small percentage of funding and a significant percentage of regulations. Finally, nearly 15,000 local school districts make policy for 90,000 public schools within the constraints set by state and federal regulators.

The reforms we consider in this section include several launched by a number of states in the 1990s and incorporated into Title I of the federal No Child Left Behind Act of 2001 (NCLB): standards-based reform, test-based accountability, and efforts to close the achievement gap. We also look at parental choice, vouchers, and charter schools, which generally trace their origins to state and local initiatives, although choice is a hallmark of NCLB. Rethinking teacher salaries (merit pay), shifting local power to the mayor (mayoral control), and delegating authority to schools (school-based management) are usually state or local initiatives.

Standards-Based Reform

With reports of a failing public education system
as their impetus, politicians and business leaders
embraced the idea that schools,
like businesses, should focus on results.

" I hope that you will join me to define national goals in education for the first time. From this day forward let us be an America of tougher standards, of higher goals, and a land of bigger dreams."

These words, spoken by President George H.W. Bush during the national education summit in 1989, launched a national movement to set high academic standards for all students.

If students, like Olympic gymnasts, were judged against a set of challenging standards for performance instead of being compared with other students, schools would improve. Parents and employers would know what students had learned, not simply that they were doing better or worse than their peers. Moreover, if *all* students were held to the same high standards, struggling students would no longer face a watered-down curriculum, in effect denying them access to higher education and better jobs. It might take more time for some students, but all would be expected to succeed. These assumptions underlie standards-based reform.

No one can be against "high standards"—that would be tantamount to supporting "low standards." Yet standards-based reform was barely out of the starting blocks before controversy erupted. Just beneath the surface were some sticky questions: What are the standards, and who chooses them? Are standards a sort of "Big Brother" measure telling everyone what to do or

what goals to shoot for? What tests measure whether students meet standards? Where is the cutoff score for meeting standards, and who sets it? Should everyone be held to the same standards, even students with limited English proficiency and those with disabilities? And what happens to students—and their schools—who do not meet the standards?

Where did the idea originate?

Spurred by reports in the mid-1980s of a failing public education system and a poor showing in international comparisons, state and national politicians and business leaders embraced the idea that schools, like businesses, should focus on results. Moreover, these leaders believed that better performance on tests would be reflected in national economic productivity down the line. They were joined by advocates for poor and minority students, who felt such youngsters were being gypped by a watered-down curriculum and poor teaching. Strange bedfellows, they rallied around standards as a strategy for increasing international economic competitiveness and equity.

Like all grand policy ideas, reality trumped the rhetoric. In the early 1990s the idea that education organizations or government-appointed committees could develop national standards fell prey to political spats and questions about the federal government's role. Criticism flew from all directions; there was agreement only that the thousands of pages of standards produced by various groups were unworkable. Schools would have to run 24 hours a day to cover everything, the critics charged.

So the imagined ideal of a few really important big ideas in each subject for different grade levels bit the dust early. But this did not slow the momentum. By 1994, several states had designed standards-based systems, and major federal legislation incorporated the ideas of standards-based reform. Congress offered funds to get all states to develop standards-based systems and introduced the phrase "high standards" into the longstanding federal education program that provides aid to disadvantaged students, Title I of the Elementary and Secondary Education Act (ESEA). By 2002, the Title I legislation, rolled into an updated ESEA dubbed the No Child Left Behind Act (NCLB), cast standards in terms of reaching "proficiency on challenging state academic achievement standards and state academic assessments."

And standards have never traveled alone. New policies from Washington and state capitals tied standards to testing and to accountability. Without tests matched to the new standards, no one would know whether students were learning everything they were supposed to learn. So new tests would be needed to replace the old one-size-fits-all norm-referenced tests already used by schools nationwide.

Accountability became the watchword of the day. State and federal policymakers offered schools greater authority and flexibility to design their programs in exchange for accepting greater responsibility for student performance. Over time, the "authority and flexibility" side of the trade didn't pan out for schools without sufficient resources and help to figure out how to do a better job. Moreover, the "responsibility" side of the trade translated into more testing with penalties for failure to meet standards. In fact, federal and state policies now have begun to decrease the

Standards have never traveled alone. Without tests matched to the new standards, no one would know whether students were learning everything they were supposed to learn.

flexibility of schools to design their own programs while increasing the accountability side of the bargain. (See Test-Based Accountability, p. 21.)

What problem is standards-based reform intended to solve?

Standards-based reform tackles nothing less than overhauling the entire public school system. Its goal, in the words of corporate and political leaders, is to create a world-class education system, overcoming the perceived failure of the current system and thereby improving the nation's global economic competitiveness. To do so, in the words of IBM's former Chairman and CEO Louis Gerstner Jr.: "We either change it all — we commit to go all the way — or we fail. There's no in between."[1]

Beyond the rhetoric, a host of solutions are embedded in the idea of standards-based reform. Standards themselves represent a sea change in thinking about achievement. In a nation wedded to comparisons and percentile rankings, standards were intended to set a mark that all children must reach.

Standards were also expected to shift the emphasis from minimum competency to proficiency. Although critics of public education pointed to lack of mastery of the basics, high standards were expected to up the ante, leading not only to mastery of basic skills but also the analysis, problem-solving, and communication skills deemed essential for 21st century jobs.

Have test scores gone up? Current data from the state and national levels provide a mixed picture. For some states in some subjects, scores have increased.

Standards-based reform also sought to shift the definition of fairness or equity from whether schools had similar resources to whether schools produced results (as measured by test scores) that showed improvement, not just overall, but for groups that usually performed poorly. Schools now report test scores by subgroups. Test-based accountability for schools and students and penalties for failure to perform adequately were intended to motivate teachers and students to work harder to reach the high standards.

Does standards-based reform work?

No doubt, standards-based reform has made an impact. Consider the substantial increase in sales of standardized tests. A snapshot here: Testing was a $263 million business in 1997, but a $924 million industry in 2004.[2] Equally prominent is the change in how results are reported. To some, this represents progress: a focus on results and attention to often-ignored subgroups, such as black and Hispanic students. To others, these same shifts represent backsliding: an overemphasis on annual standardized tests and test preparation at the expense of teaching students how to think and apply what they know. Ample research supports both viewpoints.

Have test scores gone up? Current data from the state and national levels provide a mixed picture. For some states in some subjects, scores have increased. National Assessment of Educational Progress long-term trend data from 1990 to 2004 show increases for some age groups in some subjects. For example, reading scores have increased for 9-year-olds, but not for older students. Math scores have increased for both 9- and 13-year-olds and stayed the same for 17-year-olds.[3]

It can be hard to make sense of state test results because most states report scores in terms of percent of students reaching proficiency—a direct result of standards-based reform. But what this means is different from one state to the next and often from one year to the next in the same state.

For example, in 2000, North Carolina reported that 84 percent of 4th graders reached proficiency in math, which seems terrific, while Louisiana reported only 12 percent, a lackluster showing. However, on the National Assessment of Educational Progress, North Carolina looked less stellar: only 28 percent of North Carolina's students reached proficiency. In Louisiana, 14 percent reached proficiency on the national test—close to the results on their state tests. This suggests that Louisiana had much tougher standards for performance.[4]

Given the demands of the No Child Left Behind Act to bring all students to the proficient level by 2014, states with high standards have a much longer and harder road than those with low standards. Not surprisingly, several states have already lowered their standards. For example, in 2004, Arizona rewrote the state test and lowered the passing scores for every grade and subject. To boost scores further, they provided guides to teachers on what the test would cover and made sample tests available online. Passing rates increased as much as 30 percentage points.[5] As 2014 approaches others are likely to take a similar approach. Otherwise, they will face the equivalent of a balloon payment on a mortgage.

Some states sidestep the idea of standards by declaring that the 50th percentile—the middle of the pack—is the bar for proficiency. Other times, proficiency is tied to a certain number of items answered correctly on a test. More confusing, states keep changing how they define meeting

The Goals That Paved the Way for Standards

In 1989, President George H.W. Bush gathered the nation's governors in Charlottesville, Va., for a first-ever national education summit. An outgrowth of the summit was a list of National Education Goals, which inspired the standards movement that followed. The goals stated that, by 2000:

■ All children in America will start school ready to learn.

■ The high school graduation rate will increase to at least 90 percent.

■ All students will leave grades 4, 8, and 12 having demonstrated competency over challenging subject matter in the core academic subjects.

■ U.S. students will be first in the world in mathematics and science achievement.

■ Every adult American will be literate and will possess the knowledge and skills necessary to compete in a global economy and exercise the rights and responsibilities of citizenship.

■ Every school in the United States will be free of drugs, violence, and the unauthorized presence of firearms and alcohol and will offer a disciplined environment conducive to learning.

■ The nation's teaching force will have access to programs for the continued improvement of professional skills and the opportunity to acquire the knowledge and skills needed to instruct and prepare all American students for the next century.

■ Every school will promote partnerships that will increase parental involvement and participation in promoting the social, emotional, and academic growth of children.

---

standards or reaching proficiency. These are political, not educational, decisions. No state policymaker can afford to say 90 percent of his or her state's students have failed to meet standards or reach proficiency. If the bar is too high, it will likely be lowered.

Ultimate judgments about the impact of standards-based reform will always be subject to debate because the original policy ideas have never been practiced. Instead of broad agreement on a few ambitious standards, most states have lengthy lists that enumerate every skill, reinforcing the frequent criticism of American education: a

mile wide and an inch deep. Instead of new tests that show what students know and can do, most states use the same old ones. Instead of trading flexibility for accountability, schools actually have less discretion, more testing, and stiffer penalties for low test scores than they once did. In fact, under No Child Left Behind, these schools can improve substantially and still be penalized. Finally, the idea that schools would have the resources and training needed to teach to high standards never completely gained traction among state and federal policymakers.

So the good news is that high standards for all

students coupled with reporting results by sub-groups such as student ethnicity and poverty has focused attention on bringing up those at the bottom. It keeps the public and educators aware that tremendous effort and resources are needed to accelerate the learning of the lowest-scoring students, who have the longest way to go. Standards-based reform has also zeroed in on test performance, leading in some cases to more careful tracking of the progress of individual students and better attempts to help them.

The solution…in our view

In theory, standards-based reform offers a strong starting point for strengthening public education. It can set high expectations for what students should know and be able to do and carefully track whether particular groups of students are lagging behind. So the solution is not to abandon standards or ignore the students most likely to perform poorly. Instead, the solution lies in figuring out what it takes for schools to meet high standards. The schools with the highest concentrations of minority and poor children also tend to be those with the fewest well-trained and well-seasoned teachers.[6] Simply testing these students more—and even streamlining the curriculum to prepare them for tests—is not the answer. The bold vision behind standards begs for serious attention to good teaching, strong curriculum materials, tests that truly capture what we want students to learn, and help for students who need it.

Test-Based Accountability

Schools have used standardized assessments
for nearly a century, but the standards movement
is fueling new pressures and linking
high-stakes consequences to test results.

Across the country, teachers prepare students for the state tests they will take each spring. The stakes are high. Federal legislation has made standardized tests the basis for determining whether students and schools have met the proficiency targets set by their states. Failure to meet the targets can have serious consequences: in some cases, whether a student graduates, a school is restaffed or closed, or the state takes over a district.

The rhetoric of accountability appeals to legislators and to the public: High stakes will put pressure on students and teachers to improve, scores will go up, and, as written in the federal No Child Left Behind Act of 2001 (NCLB), all students will reach proficiency by 2014. The argument begs the question of how top-down pressure to improve translates into better classroom teaching and more learning. Do scores go up? And if they do, does that signify more learning, or have teachers and students simply learned how to *play the game*—figuring out what is likely to be on the test and concentrating on those topics.

Where did high-stakes testing originate?

Standardized tests have been a staple of American public education for nearly a century. Together with teacher recommendations, test scores have been used to place students in particular programs or tracks. What is significantly different today is that nearly all states and the federal government rely on test scores alone to make high-stakes judgments about students and teachers, and penalties follow if performance does not meet targets.

This major shift in emphasis stems from the same source that launched standards-based reform: a coalition of business leaders, politicians, and policy advisers who argued that the nation's performance on international tests is tied to economic productivity. Policymakers saw the United States' low ranking on international tests relative to other countries and identified the public schools as the source of the problem. As others had done in the late 19th century, late 20th century policymakers looked to business models for reform ideas. From that view, students' test scores became products, their parents customers, and taxpayers shareholders to whom the schools are accountable for results, based on annual increases in test scores rather than profits.

In the 1990s, several states launched their own versions of high-stakes testing and accountability. Then, the No Child Left Behind Act required all states to use nationally standardized tests and to set proficiency targets for most grade levels— called Adequate Yearly Progress (AYP)—and for subgroups of students (for example, racial/ethnic groups and students with disabilities). States and districts are expected to help schools that fail to meet their targets and to provide alternative choices or extra services for students if their parents request them. Schools that continue to fail face more serious sanctions, including closure. Failing state tests required for high school graduation has equally serious consequences for individual students.

What problem is high-stakes testing intended to solve?

"Accountability tests allow parents to know whether or not their children are truly learning. They are the key to unmasking problems in a system that for too long has allowed too many children to pass through without learning the basics needed to succeed."[7] This statement by U.S. Rep. John Boehner, a Republican from Ohio, captures the broad sweep of problems that high-stakes testing is expected to solve. Parents want information on how their children are doing and how they stack up against others while national and state policymakers seek big-picture accountability. However, test scores that point to weak spots in the public school system—which policymakers want to know about—do not tell individual parents anything about what or how much their child is learning. Nor do they give teachers the kind of information they need to improve their instruction for individual students.

When penalties are attached to tests, according to researchers, the tests become the curriculum. In fact, what is not on the test gets ignored. Whether this is bad or good depends on whether the tests do what policymakers believe they do. The use of tests for high-stakes accountability assumes that tests measure what parents and teachers expect students to learn, the public agrees on the definition of "proficient" (or, how good is good enough?), and what tests measure is what schools teach, not a student's educational background.

It's actually quite difficult to meet these assumptions, it turns out. No single test can measure everything. Standardized tests measure what policymakers and test designers think is important. Tests are given in some subjects, but not others. They cover topics familiar to everyone (e.g., grammar, spelling, comprehension), but the items are chosen for technical reasons. For example, no item is included that everyone is likely to get right, and much of what is learned in school is not tested. Even when publishers declare their tests to be "aligned" to state standards, they can only address a tiny percent of the hundreds and hundreds of standards.

So testing experts like University of California, Los Angeles emeritus professor James Popham and University of Colorado professor Robert Linn argue that standardized tests should not be used to judge school or teacher quality. They were originally created to show how students stack up against each other—not how much they have learned in school. Even when such tests claim to be "standards based" the types of questions and criteria for inclusion are similar. Measuring school quality with a standardized test is "like measuring temperature with a tablespoon," according to Popham—a purpose for which it was not intended and does a dreadful job.[8]

Because NCLB requires each state to define what it means by "proficient," the assumption that the public agrees on how good is good enough has been put to the test. Each state picks a cutoff point for defining proficiency. In fall 2003 the percent of schools that failed to meet Adequate Yearly Progress (AYP) mandates ranged from 8 percent in Minnesota to 87 percent in Florida.[9] This does not mean that some states have very high proportions of proficient students and others do not. It means that their definitions of proficiency differ.

Most states do not pick cutoff points based on consensus about what it means to be proficient. The choice is made by a state-level committee based on a best guess of how many students will fail or on actual test results. When they misjudge, the cutoff score changes. In Pennsylvania, for example, the state lowered the threshold for schools in 2004. Without the change, more than twice as many schools would have failed to meet the target.[10] In some states, cutoff scores determine whether a student can graduate from high school. Here, too, states retreat when faced with high rates of failure. For example, after high failure rates on New York state's new rigorous math exam in 2003, the results were set aside and the score for passing lowered.

The final assumption underlying high-stakes testing is that schools control what the tests measure. This is the trickiest assumption of all.

The goal of high-stakes testing, as embodied in NCLB, is to ensure that all students reach proficiency. Yet students start school at very different places; some can already read, others do not know the alphabet. Some can count to 100; others cannot count to 10. Moreover, students from families living in poverty, which are disproportionately minority families, are far more likely to be among those who start school behind their peers and often fall further and further behind.

The goal of NCLB is to pressure schools to make sure these students reach proficiency instead of falling behind. But this creates several challenges for schools: On the good side, reporting test scores by groups defined by race, poverty, language, and disability ensures that these students are not overlooked. At the same time, these students are the most likely to have low scores, bringing down overall scores for their schools, as well. So schools with higher proportions of such students are less likely to meet their targets, even those with excellent teaching. Moreover, the more diverse the student population, the harder it is to meet the standard because it must be met by so many different subgroups.

To set the same high expectations for all students, the law prescribes measuring students each year against a fixed standard (for example, percent scoring above the 50th percentile). Yet this approach masks strong gains in scores made by students who start very low, but still do not reach the standard, frustrating both students and teachers.[11]

Allowing no excuses for poor-performing students sends an important message to educators;

The goal of high-stakes testing is to ensure that all students reach proficiency. Yet students start school at very different places; some can already read, others do not know the alphabet.

many teachers have for too long harbored low expectations for some students and simply given up on them. Yet high expectations are not enough when teachers lack skills, students are unwilling, and parents cannot lend support.

These problems are not easily resolved. They point to the enormous responsibility placed on the public school system and the challenges schools face in meeting the high expectations of the nation. The question is whether the trade-offs embodied in high-stakes accountability do more good than harm or vice versa.

Does high-stakes testing work?

Does external pressure on students and teachers to improve translate into better teaching and more learning? The simple answer is yes—and no. If the question is whether the scores go up, the answer is often yes. If the question is whether the tests by themselves improve teaching and learning, the answer is usually no.

Scores on high-stakes tests for elementary schools typically increase the first few years they are in place. Whether these increases reflect more learning is less certain. Teachers and students become more familiar with the test and how to prepare for it. To find out if higher scores on high-stakes tests reflect more learning, researchers compare results with other tests such as the National Assessment of Educational Progress. This sounds simple, but it turns out that the answer depends on how it's done.[12]

High-stakes tests do influence what teachers do, researchers find. Teachers pay more attention to what they expect to be on the test and less attention to areas not tested. After Washington state launched its test, teachers reported spending more time on reading and math and less on social studies, science, the arts, and physical education, which were not tested.[13]

Similarly, NCLB's insistence on reporting scores for all subgroups of students calls attention to students who might otherwise be ignored when only schoolwide averages are reported.

These benefits also carry costs. The higher the stakes, the more teaching becomes preparation for the test, and the more the test becomes the curriculum. This narrow goal can exclude not only entire subject areas, but also minimize attention to intellectual and social goals highly valued by parents and educators and future employers.

When state tests require writing and explanations of problem-solving, "test prep" is of a higher caliber than preparation for multiple-choice fact-based questions. Some states are moving in this direction, but others, such as Maryland, have reversed course given the high costs of scoring items that are not multiple choice. Even when the tests are better, the teaching may not be because teachers are less well-prepared. In the 1990s, studies of states with new kinds of tests, such as Kentucky and Maryland, found teachers trying to teach to more complicated tests designed to get at students' understanding of concepts, but the teachers themselves didn't know enough to do a good job of explaining the ideas.[14]

High-stakes accountability is "good for bad teachers and bad for good teachers," according to a mentor-teacher in an Arizona elementary school who was interviewed by a researcher in 2002. For

Testing At Its Best and Worst

	The Good	The Bad	The Ugly
Teachers	What's on the test can lead teachers to teach things they have ignored and to teach kids they have ignored	Teachers don't know what to do so they resort to test prep and attention to the kids just below standard	Pressure to increase scores leads to cheating, and teachers ignore struggling students whose scores are unlikely to rise
Students	Some students try harder when tests are tied to a course grade or promotion	Students don't learn important skills and knowledge	Students give up and drop out
Schools	Principals and teachers work together to figure out how to raise test scores	Nothing is taught except what is on the test. The curriculum becomes 'test prep'	Principals and teachers leave low-performing (poor) schools to go to higher-performing (wealthier) schools
Districts	District leaders pay attention to all the schools and help them improve	District leaders don't know how to help schools improve	The state takes over failing schools but doesn't know how to help them improve

teachers who have been doing little in the way of teaching, high-stakes testing can prod them into action. They will not turn into good teachers without considerable training and help, but they will teach. But for those who have been working hard at the job, the pressure can turn into anxiety and frustration over the limits of test preparation and their ability to teach other things, and simply not knowing what else to do to raise test scores.

Moreover, anxiety about high-stakes tests leads to troublesome results: in the worst-case scenarios, teachers and students cheat, students give up and drop out, or teachers leave poor schools for those with higher-performing students. For example, in 2004, the *Dallas Morning News* conducted an analysis of scores on the Texas Assessment of Knowledge and Skills (TAKS) and found "strong evidence of organized, teacher-led cheating on the TAKS test in dozens of Texas schools and suspicious scores in hundreds more."[15] A Cato Institute report claims that NCLB "obviously increases the incentives for cheating" and anticipates more in the future, "both detected and undetected."[16]

The real "test" of high-stakes testing is to be found in the remedies applied when schools or students fail. Do the consequences attached to poor performance actually improve teaching and learning? Standardized test scores do not provide teachers with any guidance on what they should do differently. States and districts are expected to help, but most lack enough people with the expertise to do the job. New programs and different textbooks may solve part of the problem, but a long history of research proves that programs are only as good as the people who put them into practice. Many great-sounding solutions—even those proved effective in other settings—founder when tried in new situations.

If districts fail to help schools, states are expected to take over. Yet states have no proven track record of being able to do this successfully, and there are numerous examples of failures. Even closing low-performing schools and re-opening them with new staff has not proved successful. In California and Maryland, such actions did not lead to improvement; in fact, some schools were worse off.[17]

The same reasons that caused low performance in the first place do not disappear with different faces at the helm.

The solution...in our view

Testing is not going away, but both the tests and the ways they are used can be greatly improved.

Proponents of standards-based reform emphasize the importance of good tests—tests that are closely tied to a reasonable set of standards and that go beyond multiple-choice items. Such tests are typically not those sold by national testing companies. One direction for improvement would be to break the stranglehold of a handful of national test publishers and invest in the development of better tests—tests that probe whether a student can ask good questions, set up an experiment, debate an issue, create a product, stick with a difficult task, and work with others.

Tests also should be used for the purposes for which they were designed. Policymakers need to monitor progress in schools, but they do not need information on every student in every subject. Like political polls and customer surveys, testing samples of students can monitor progress at lower cost and without the negative effects of high-stakes testing on individuals. No matter how good or how appropriate the test, however, decisions about the future of a student or a school should be based on more than one test score. Test scores are not perfectly accurate. They have margins of error like poll results and should be reported the same way. Because tests are imperfect, a student should not be denied a diploma on the basis of one exam. Nor should a single score determine a school's success or failure.

Better tests, used more appropriately, are a start, but only that. At the end of the day, the question is whether schools can get what they need to improve. External pressure may be an effective motivator for some, but it does not tell principals and teachers what they should do to raise student achievement.

Closing the Achievement Gap

Policymakers are paying increased attention to eliminating disparities in achievement between groups of students, but there are dangers in making generalizations about how certain students perform.

Picture a 5th grade classroom in San Diego. The 33 students range from six newcomers who arrived from Mexico mid-year and speak no English, to Latino and Hmong students who speak a little English, to white and Latino students who are fluent in English and high-performing. The teacher struggles to provide challenging materials to his top students and to accelerate the learning of those at the bottom, hoping to close the achievement gap inside his classroom.

Imagine two schools in Chicago, one with all African-American students from poor South Side families and the other with mostly affluent white students on the North Side. The principal of the South Side school knows his test scores will be much lower than the North Side school and wonders how he can increase test scores enough to begin to close the gap. Most of his entering kindergartners are unable to hold a pencil or recognize letters of the alphabet, while 5-year-olds at the North Side school can already recognize many words and some can read.

Whether comparing students in a classroom or comparing schools in a district or comparing one district with another, achievement gaps among racial and economic groups persist. The intent behind closing these gaps is to break the connection between race or family income and achievement, while at the same time continuing to improve the performance of the top students. For

this to happen, the achievement of the lowest-performing students must increase at a much higher rate than those at the top. As in a race, those at the back of the pack have to run much faster than those in the lead to catch up.

Gaps between test score averages for black and Hispanic students, at the low end, and white students, at the high end, have persisted for decades. The same gaps fall between the poorest students and their more affluent peers. The gaps also show up in the rates for dropping out, taking college-prep courses, graduating from high school, and obtaining college degrees, and ultimately in the jobs the students get.

Real estate agents and scholars know that test scores reflect the wealth of a school's neighborhood. Well-to-do neighborhoods have schools with high test scores. In the United States, black and Hispanic families are more likely to be poor than white families and therefore their children are more likely to post lower test scores. In fact, more than one-third of all African-American children (43 percent) live in poverty as do 30 percent of Hispanic children, compared with 10 percent of white children.[18]

To make matters worse, schools with mostly minority and poor students have fewer experienced teachers and fewer supplies than those with more affluent white students. The same problem exists within schools: those performing least well are the most likely to get inexperienced teachers and low-level instruction. As one advocate put it: "We take kids who have less to begin with, and then we give them less in school, too."[19]

It is no surprise that test scores are more likely to be at the low end for both minority students and those from the least-wealthy families. The challenge is what to do about it.

Where did the idea of closing the achievement gap originate?

Achievement gaps between minority and white students and between poor and more affluent students have been documented for as long as the tools to measure them have existed. From 1970 to 2004, the gaps narrowed somewhat for some age groups, but the point spread remains large. For example, in spite of 33 years of slowly increasing reading scores, black children have lower scores in 2004 than white children had in 1971.[20] The story is the same for Hispanic students.

The achievement gap reflects disparities in children's backgrounds upon starting school—disparities which are then compounded by the gaps in funding, teacher expertise, and curriculum rigor that children encounter in school. Those who start the farthest behind usually attend schools with the fewest resources or are relegated to tracks within schools that offer the weakest academic program. As a result, the gap between poor children and their better-off peers increases as students move through school.

What is distinctly different today is the attention to achievement gaps and the dual beliefs among policymakers that all children can reach proficiency and, with enough effort, schools alone can close the gaps. In response, "closing the gap" has become a mantra in schools and districts across the country.

This renewed attention results from state and federal requirements to report test results by racial groups and the specific requirement in the federal No Child Left Behind Act that each group must show progress. The design of NCLB is modeled

Achievement gaps between minority and white students and between poor and more affluent students have been documented for as long as the tools to measure them have existed. What's different now is the attention to those gaps.

after Texas reforms launched in the 1980s at the prodding of businessman H. Ross Perot. Those reforms required annual testing and reporting results by racial groups. In the 1990s, then-Governor George W. Bush introduced a new Texas test and by the end of decade proclaimed that scores had climbed and achievement gaps were closing. [21]

But achievement gaps are averages, and averages can be dangerous. As statisticians are fond of saying: You can drown walking across a creek with an average depth of one foot. Many white students score lower than many black students. Many Hispanic students score higher than many white students. One danger in reporting data by racial group is the potential to reinforce stereotypes, encouraging educators to judge students based on race rather than individual learning needs.

What problem is closing the achievement gap intended to solve?

Closing the achievement gap represents the promise of America—providing equitable opportunities for all Americans to reach their full potential. The public schools serve as the primary venue, outside the family, for getting a shot at a college degree and a high-paying job. That some youngsters would do better than others has always been taken for granted. The dream is that those differences are not tied to race or social class.

Under standards-based reform, the goal of equitable opportunity has been restated. The aim is to ensure that all students reach a certain level of proficiency, based on each state's definition of proficiency. The challenge school systems face is how to close the gap without limiting what top students learn and without setting the bar so low that everyone can pass it.

Does focusing attention on closing the achievement gap work?

Federal and state requirements to report achievement test scores by racial groups—and require progress for each—has been remarkably successful in drawing attention to achievement gaps. Educators and education policymakers all talk about the achievement gap—language that was noticeably absent in recent years. "We're doing CTAG [closing the achievement gap]," one California superintendent said during a 2005 meeting of superintendents and researchers. The problem cannot be swept under the rug. Achievement gaps exist and need attention.

Whether paying more attention to achievement gaps results in narrowing them is not so clear. Even where such evidence is touted, it is rarely sustained and confirmed by other data sources. For example, an elementary school might demonstrate a smaller gap between white and Hispanic students this year compared with last year, but only in 2nd grade reading or 4th grade math. Moreover, the following year the gap may not continue to decrease. Still, attention to gaps is a first step, and any progress deserves celebration.

Repeated studies show that it is possible for some schools to narrow achievement gaps. Studies that identify schools that "beat the odds"—those with mostly minority and poor students—inspire hope by demonstrating what is possible. But the number that have done so consistently, over several years at most grade levels, is quite small and virtually nonexistent beyond elementary

school. Moreover, what is learned from these schools runs up against the perennial problem of other school reforms: how to take ideas that work in one place and successfully transplant them in others.

Gaps also narrow or widen for reasons that have nothing to do with real improvements. Lowering a cutoff score can make it look as if gaps are narrowing, but it won't be because of more learning by students at the bottom. Yet states are under enormous pressure to get more students to proficiency each year. Abigail Thernstrom, a member of the Massachusetts board of education, predicted that it would be impossible even in a dozen years for all students to reach the state's proficiency level, which is roughly comparable to the definition of proficient under NAEP, the National Assessment of Educational Progress. "It's a ludicrous goal," she said. "We will have to define proficiency way down—I mean way, way down."[22]

The solution…in our view

Under NCLB, schools are expected not only to keep achievement gaps from widening, but also to make up for whatever gaps exist when children enter school. This is a tall order.

It's not hard to see that the lowest-performing students cannot catch up without much more time to learn and better instruction. More time means instruction after school and during the summer without sacrificing other important learning goals. Better instruction means better teachers, more efficient use of time, and solid lessons. This means getting the best teachers and materials to the students who need them the most.

Getting the best to poor and minority students, especially when budgets are tight, can end up pitting wealthier, politically connected parents who also want the best for their children against poor parents with less political muscle. Does the public will exist to move the best teachers and the best equipment to the schools in the poorest neighborhoods? "The solution seems obvious," said Texas District Judge John Dietz in his 2004 ruling on school funding in Texas. "Texas needs to close the education gap. But the rub is that it costs money to close the educational achievement gap."[23]

Even choosing a good curriculum uncovers disagreements about what that means. Arguments continue over whether the best is a highly structured, skills-based, teacher-proof curriculum or one that is child-centered and designed to motivate children and prod their thinking, or some combination of both.[24]

Many question whether schools alone can bridge the achievement gap, even with additional resources. It is one thing to have high hopes for all students. It is another to know how to dramatically speed up learning so struggling students catch up to their peers. Schools certainly have a role to play, but most scholars and policy analysts agree that efforts to close the gap must begin much earlier than kindergarten and outside the school. Without tackling the barriers to learning outside of school, educators' efforts can only go so far.

In its proclamations on closing the achievement gap, the National Governors Association emphasizes the importance of the first five years of a child's life, arguing that the need for young children to have stable, nurturing relationships, access to health care and proper nutrition, and early exposure to learning activities is paramount. Specifically, NGA recommends high-quality child care, professional development for caregivers, preschool programs, health care and social services, and parent education, among other items.[25]

Closing the gap cannot happen quickly, easily, or cheaply. It requires a balancing act: providing funds and keeping pressure on schools to expect the most from the least well-off students without setting unrealistic expectations and punishing schools for failing to meet them.

Schools certainly have a role to play, but most scholars and policy analysts agree that efforts to close the gap must begin much earlier than kindergarten and outside the school. For one, high-quality child care is crucial.

Parental Choice

Parents can now turn to an array of options for their children's educations, including charters, vouchers, and for-profit schools. Yet few choose to leave their neighborhood schools.

"An escape hatch from broken systems." So goes the rhetoric of those promoting charters and vouchers. And they have found a sympathetic ear among many urban parents and reformers who fear that large urban districts are beyond repair and poor minority students are being left behind.

Arguing that the public schools should operate like a market, proponents of vouchers, charters, and for-profit schools claim that expanded choices will spur urban schools to improve, as they compete for students who can choose among alternatives. Parental choice has a long history, but only recently have the options become decidedly market-based and officially sanctioned in federal and state laws. At the same time, sharp and nasty conflict has dominated debates over using parental choice as a tool to revamp low-performing schools.

Giving options to parents who feel their children are trapped in lousy neighborhood schools has broad support, but creates a new set of concerns. Parents in Dayton, Ohio, can choose from nearly 50 charter schools—more such schools than in the entire state of New Jersey—that enroll 26 percent of public school students in the district. "Never in a million years did I think we'd end up with 50 charters in a community of this size," a former president of the Dayton board of education told a reporter in 2005. "We're developing two complete and competing public systems."[26] Parents in South Philadelphia frustrated with their local school can choose to send their children to an independent public charter school on the other side of town, a science magnet school a short bus ride away, or a nearby for-profit Edison school that provides computers for each and every student.[27]

Because charter school founders receive the same funding per child that traditional public schools receive, issues of money and accountability loom large. "Most charters were started for the wrong reason—to make money," a founder of one in Scottsdale, Ariz., said to a reporter in 2002, "and most of them are mediocre."[28] And, many critics fear that the reform hurts public schools by drawing scarce funds away from the rest of the school system.

Other critics worry that putting market forces to work in a public system elevates the individual family's interests over the larger purposes served by tax-supported schools, such as developing good citizens, promoting shared social values, and equipping students with the skills to thrive in an ever-changing economy.

Where did the choice idea originate?

Although parental choice attracted lots of attention in the early 1990s, its roots date back 150 years and are deeply embedded in democratic principles. In the mid-19th century, Midwestern

German parents got their school boards to establish schools that would conduct instruction in their native language. At about the same time, many urban Catholics wanted their schools to inculcate religious values and left public schools to establish private ones. In 1925, the U.S. Supreme Court prohibited states from requiring every student to attend public schools, thus making private schools and parental choice constitutional.[29]

By the 1960s and 1970s, liberals promoted parental choice through vouchers—or government-issued payments to cover tuition—because of their deep concern over ghetto-bound parents having to send their children to ineffective urban schools. Under some desegregation court orders, districts also established "magnet" schools focusing on special curricula where parents could choose to send their children instead of neighborhood schools. And in the mid-1980s, conservatives championed vouchers, charter schools, and other forms of parental choice for the poor.

Even at the height of this interest in private schools and choices within the public school system, more than 90 percent of American children attended public school. Nonetheless, an established tradition of parental choice anchored in the U.S. Constitution had emerged.

After many battles in the past decade, supporters of parental choice have slowly carved out a solid niche within the nation's nearly 90,000 public schools. More than 3,600 public charter schools enrolled more than 1 million children in 40 states and Washington, D.C. in 2005. Fifty-nine for-profit companies (called education management organizations or EMOs) in 24 states and the District of Columbia managed 535 public schools (many of which are charters) with 239,000 students that year.[30]

Six states (Colorado, Wisconsin, Ohio, Florida, Maine, and Vermont) have passed voucher laws that give eligible parents checks to enroll their sons and daughters in public or private schools.

Conflicts over choice will continue, particularly when the dollars to support alternatives draw from the same purse that funds public schools.

(The Florida Supreme Court, however, declared that state's law unconstitutional in January 2006.) Milwaukee and Cleveland offer publicly funded vouchers to low-income families to enroll their children in private schools, including religious ones, and the U.S. Supreme Court found such programs constitutional. Moreover, the U.S. Government Accountability Office found in 2002 that privately funded voucher programs awarded nearly $60 million in tuition to about 46,000 students.[31]

Parental choice is also embedded in the federal No Child Left Behind Act. The law states that parents of students in failing schools can transfer to higher-performing schools or request tutoring from a private provider at school expense. Ultimately, if the school continues to fail, a state can take over the school and outsource the school's management to a for-profit company, convert it into a charter school, or operate the school itself. [32]

What problem is parental choice intended to solve?

Providing better options for parents trapped in lousy schools, stimulating innovation by freeing schools from the regulatory stranglehold of districts, and improving urban schools through competition are all problems that choice-based reformers claim to solve. Market-oriented reformers and business leaders believe public schools are an inefficient and ineffective monopoly that must be broken up. They promote vouchers, EMOs, and charter schools as ways of freeing urban schools from their regulatory stranglehold and giving poor parents a chance to send their children to other, better schools. Moreover, injecting competition into big-city districts where parents can choose among different options would jolt boards of education and superintendents, fearful of losing students and state funds, into working harder to improve all urban schools, proponents say.

At the same time, choice-based reforms raise a new set of problems. One is the conversion of public schools into private ones funded by public money.[33] Another is depleting already strapped urban schools of funds desperately needed to attract qualified staff, refurbish facilities, and hold staff accountable for upgrading low performance.

As heated as the struggle over vouchers, charter schools, and EMOs has been in the past decade, both promoters and opponents agree that parental involvement in their children's schooling increases the chances of their children doing better academically. Both sides also agree that large urban districts fail to offer poor parents the high-quality schooling that middle- and upper-income families secure when they buy homes in those suburbs or neighborhoods with strong public schools. Even with such agreement, conflicts over parental choice as a school reform will continue, particularly when the dollars to support vouchers, charter schools, and for-profit companies draw from the same purse that funds all public schools.

Does parental choice work?

One way to answer the question is to ask: Has choice increased the options available to poor parents? Parents in New York City; Dayton, Ohio; Washington, D.C.; Philadelphia; Seattle; Milwaukee; Cleveland; and other places where charter schools and vouchers are available do have more choices now. For most poor parents, however, the answer is no. In spite of the hullabaloo over choice-based options, less than 3

percent of all public schoolchildren attended these schools of choice as of 2004. In other words, 97 percent of public school parents still send their children to regular public schools.

If more choices were available, would poor parents choose one? Under NCLB, in schools that have not gotten better, parents can switch to another school in the same district. Yet no more than 2 percent of the eligible parents in 2002-03 and 2003-04 have used this provision of the law. The low response rate may be due to parents' lack of information about this part of the law, the scarcity of better schools in the district, parents' preferences for the neighborhood school, or some combination of these reasons.[34]

Another question is whether voucher, charter school, or for-profit EMOs are better options for parents than the urban schools they are designed to replace. Like urban schools, schools of choice vary considerably. Some are fine schools; others are dreadful. Many suffer from the same problems that beset urban districts. For example, Ohio's charter schools lose more than half their teachers each year and most leave teaching altogether.[35]

In terms of test scores, there is no clear winner. Some studies of vouchers, charters, and EMOs claim that children do better in the choice schools. Other studies reject those claims and show students in public schools outscoring those in charter, EMO, or voucher-based schools. [36]

Choice advocates and opponents dispute the research design, sample selection, methodologies used, and quality of the evidence of these studies. Depending upon how much weight readers give to these technical issues, the mixed findings hardly bang the drums loudly for vouchers, charter schools, or for-profits. For the immediate future, no clear answer to the effectiveness of parental choice can be found in research.

Finally, this question: Have districts that established charter schools, EMOs, and voucher programs responded to the resulting competition by reducing the number of low-performing schools and increasing the ranks of high-performing ones? Here again, the evidence is mixed. Some researchers claim that district officials, fearing the loss of state funds, have introduced novel programs to stem the flow of students either to voucher-accepting schools or newly chartered ones. Other researchers have found little evidence of districts with many charter schools and EMOs launching initiatives to retain students in existing schools. [37]

At best, then, the principle of choice and competition as advocated by reformers has yet to show persuasive evidence of parents exercising choice, unvarnished academic success, or public school transformation. Of course, research and evaluation studies seldom determine the worth of a reform. Politics and judicial decisions move policymakers and parents quicker and further than findings from researchers' investigations. The U.S. Supreme Court's *Zelman* v. *Simmons-Harris* (2002) decision declaring that Cleveland's voucher program was constitutional, for example, directly led Colorado to establish a voucher program less than a year later. The political popularity of charter schools and EMOs as alternatives for minority students, teachers, and parents seeking customized options nearly guarantees that few elected officials will rescind legislation authorizing these choices.[38]

The solution…in our view

Because choice-based reforms serve a limited number of parents and show inconclusive results, solutions must follow two paths. One is that urban schools still serve and will continue to serve the vast majority of children. Whatever their problems, it is unconscionable to turn away from attempting to improve these blighted schools, no matter how hard the task. The other path is to ensure that schools receiving public money, whether private or public, receive the same scrutiny, are held to the same standards, and provide the same safeguards against discriminatory practices found in traditional public schools.

Regardless of the numbers or the research,

The political popularity of charter schools and EMOs as alternatives for minority students, teachers, and parents seeking options nearly guarantees that few elected officials will rescind laws authorizing these choices.

parental choice as a school reform has staying power because of its roots in the history of school reform and democratic practices. Both tradition and court decisions preserve the principles that parents can send their children to private school, as 10 percent did in 2002,[39] or home school their children, as 2 percent did so in 2003.[40] Parents are not required to send their children to public schools and can choose among public schools.

Choice could spread among low-income, minority parents in big cities who seek the options that their wealthier neighbors possess. However, this is unlikely unless, for example, the NCLB provisions allowing parents to switch from a failing school were expanded to permit them to send their children to high-performing schools in adjacent districts with transportation costs fully covered by the state. Giving low-income parents dissatisfied with their children's schooling options that are superior to the neighborhood school is consistent with the tradition and democratic principles embedded in parental choice.

Merit Pay for Teachers

The idea is simple: Pay teachers based on performance, not just years of service. So, why have so many school systems turned away from this idea, and why does it keep resurfacing?

Pay-for-performance is as American as apple pie. Individuals who produce more—earn more. Those who sell shoes, homes, and life insurance get paid commissions and bonuses on the basis of how much they sell. In commercial laundries, the number of shirts ironed determines how much pay the worker gets. Even doctors in a Minneapolis-based health plan receive bonuses if their diabetic patients get blood sugar and cholesterol below certain levels, stop smoking, and take aspirin daily. Business leaders and managers have known for decades that cash incentives can motivate employees to perform at their highest levels. Why not teachers?[41]

For every year a teacher teaches, she gets an incremental raise. If she earns an advanced degree or a certificate for a teaching specialty, she receives another increase. After 15 or 20 years, teachers top out in most district salary schedules, except for occasional small, longevity increases marking 25 and 30 years of service.

Such salary plans prize experience and taking lots of university courses. A predictable salary schedule allows teachers to plan for the future and provides a degree of security. Moreover, a uniform schedule avoids pitting teacher against teacher in seeking favor with administrators who evaluate their performance: It encourages teachers to cooperate with one another rather than to compete.

Uniform salary schedules have a downside. The system of compensation assumes that all teachers are effective. It provides no incentive for teachers to reach beyond their grasp or to innovate since all teachers—mediocre and high-performing—are paid the same as long as they exceed the threshold of acceptable classroom performance. Perversely, a uniform schedule encourages experienced, effective teachers to transfer out of low-performing, largely minority schools where workplace conditions are difficult to affluent schools where teaching conditions are more attractive and they can receive the same salary they earned at the tougher school.[42]

Thus, merit-pay plans, or paying teachers for results, appeal to policymakers looking to reward effective teachers and to penalize slackers and inadequate teaching. Reformers view merit pay as a way to motivate individual teachers to excel. At the same time, it places heightened responsibility on those who evaluate classroom practice. Merit pay requires principals, other administrators, and, in some instances, other teachers to make individual judgments on classroom practice and appraisals of student performance.

Where did the merit-pay idea originate?

In the early 20th century, teachers earned whatever school boards decided to pay them. Salaries were set arbitrarily and often depended upon personal contacts, not classroom performance or how much students learned. Because there was little predictability or fairness in such an arbitrary system of compensation, school reformers, seeking to provide security to teachers in an emerging profession, introduced the uniform salary schedule in the 1920s.

Since then, nearly all teachers have been paid on schedules that rewarded experience and credentials, not performance. Pay-for-performance plans have emerged frequently in the past half-century, particularly in moments of growing dissatisfaction with public schools for producing inadequate high school graduates. During the Cold War, for example, the Soviet Union's launching of the satellite Sputnik in 1957 prompted critics to lambaste public schools for failing to produce more engineers, mathematicians, and scientists than their rival. Among the many post-Sputnik school reforms adopted was merit pay for teachers. About 10 percent of school districts in the nation embraced such plans. Within a few years, however, most had dropped them.[43]

In the past decade, mounting public displeasure with low-performing schools, especially in big cities, led critics to borrow business practices and press for teacher pay-for-performance plans. For example, at the National Education Summit in 1999, governors, top business leaders, and educators pledged to work "through statewide coalitions and local partnerships [to] ... help interested school systems and teacher organizations in ... states incorporate pay-for-performance incentive plans into their salary structures, based on lessons learned from the private sector." In this instance, teacher performance was to be measured in gains students made in achievement test scores.[44]

Since then, different merit-based plans rewarding individuals and groups of teachers for improving student achievement have been initiated in Chattanooga, Tenn.; Minneapolis; and Denver. In other districts such as Fairfax County, Va., plans were adopted and later dropped; pay-for-performance plans were rejected in Iowa and Cincinnati.

The prevailing assumption that more money will motivate teachers to teach better and thereby produce increased student learning is widely held. However, many teachers remain wary of merit-pay plans.

In the above instances, teachers' unions have stood on both sides of the merit-pay question, either endorsing or opposing plans that linked student test scores to compensation. Denver's plan, called ProComp, was initiated by the school board and superintendent, developed in close cooperation with the teachers' union, and begun as an experiment in 1999. It gained the support of most Denver teachers and subsequently, in fall 2005, city voters approved a tax referendum to support it. It was due to be implemented for all of the city's new teachers in 2006. Yet in New York City and the state of California where the mayor and governor respectively proposed merit pay, teachers' unions in both places quickly took out ads opposing the plans.[45]

The prevailing assumption that more money will motivate teachers to teach better and thereby produce increased student learning is widely shared among policymakers—recall that both presidential candidates pushed merit pay in 2004. However, teachers are wary, knowing of previous failed attempts to impose plans that ended up unfairly rewarding some teachers, especially when student test results are used to determine pay. Regardless of teacher concerns, however, more school systems will pay attention to payment-for-results now, since the No Child Left Behind Act authorizes states to provide funds for districts seeking to introduce merit pay.[46]

Merit Pay: The Denver Story

In 2004, the Denver Classroom Teachers Association voted to dump a traditional salary schedule based on years of experience and college credits and to endorse a new merit-pay plan that includes bonuses for teachers who raise students' test scores. Shortly afterward, a mayor-led coalition of civic, business, and educational leaders spent more than $1 million to promote a ballot measure to underwrite—at a cost of $25 million—a pay plan called ProComp. The measure passed in fall 2005.

So, how did this uncommon civic, business, and educator partnership succeed where others have failed?

The answer can be found in joint leadership and planning, much patience, and attention to teacher concerns. Teachers' union leaders worked closely with top school officials for six years. With the help of private funding and careful planning, the union and administration agreed to a four-year pilot project incorporating elements of pay for performance in 16 of the district's 130-plus schools. Most teachers who participated in the pilot have earned $1,500 for meeting performance objectives they had set. Teachers and administrators analyzed glitches that left some teachers angry and a revised Professional Compensation System for Teachers, or ProComp, emerged with a two-year implementation beginning in 2006.

ProComp offers teachers a menu of choices. They can earn additional money—a percentage of the starting yearly pay for a credentialed teacher (almost $33,000)—by acquiring new skills and knowledge in their teaching field, receiving satisfactory evaluations, demonstrating growth in student achievement, or working in schools with children from poor families. Current teachers have six years to decide whether to join ProComp; new teachers enter the plan automatically.

For 10-year veteran math teacher Taylor Betz who works at a low-income middle school earning just over $45,000 a year, ProComp offers a financial incentive. Under the current salary schedule, her annual pay increases would end after 13 years, except for small bumps every five years. At that rate, after 30 years of teaching, she would be making $57,190. Should she join ProComp, however, and continue to teach math in a low-income school, gather professional development credits for courses, and meet her annual goals, she could collect $3,000 to $4,000 yearly increases, taking her up to $100,000 in salary after 30 years.

"Teachers doing hard work in the hardest places deserve to be rewarded," Betz told *Teacher Magazine* in 2004, though she was quick to add that the money wasn't what motivated her. "I've chosen to do this regardless of pay," she said. "Where [the plan] will hopefully help is reducing teacher turnover within any school with a low socioeconomic profile."

SOURCES:
• Bess Keller, "Teacher Vote on Merit Pay Down to Wire," *Education Week*, March 17, 2004; pp. 1, 22-23.
• Bess Keller, "Denver Teachers Approve Pay-for-Performance Plan," *Education Week*, March 23, 2004, Web-only article, www.edweek.org/ew/articles/2004/03/23/28denver_web.h23.html
• Kerby Meyers, "Performance Anxiety," *Teacher Magazine* November 2004, pp. 15-19.

What problem is merit pay intended to solve?

Pushing (unsuccessfully) for a state referendum for merit pay, California Gov. Arnold Schwarzenegger said in his 2005 "State of the State" Address:

"[For] $50 billion [in the budget] ... we still have 30 percent of high school students not graduating. That is a human disaster. Fifty billion dollars and we still have hundreds of schools that are failing. That is an institutional disaster. Fifty billion dollars and the majority of our students cannot even perform at their grade level. That is an educational disaster. We must reward — we must financially reward — good teachers and expel those who are not. The more we reward excellent teachers, the more our teachers will be excellent. The more we tolerate ineffective teachers, the more our teachers will be ineffective. So ... I propose that a teacher's pay be tied to merit, not tenure. And I propose that a teacher's employment be tied to performance, not just showing up."[47]

Like the governor, advocates believe that merit pay will eliminate a salary schedule that rewards longevity, protects mediocre teachers, and denies skillful teachers their due recognition. Second, they say it will motivate teachers to improve and, as a result, raise the performance of their students and underperforming U.S. schools.

Does merit pay work?

Little evidence exists that the basic assumption driving merit pay systems is true. For example, paying teachers for student performance on tests did not work in late-19th Century Great Britain when Parliament mandated it. In its more than three decades there, many problems arose, including improper allocation of funds, widespread cheating, and constricted forms of teaching, which led to the system's demise.[48]

In the United States since the 1920s most merit-pay plans in public schools were enthusiastically adopted but disappeared within a few years. The

In the United States since the 1920s most merit-pay plans in public schools were enthusiastically adopted but disappeared within a few years.

reasons for adoption or disappearance seldom had to do with the position teachers' unions took. After all, in examining private schools where few unions exist, researchers found few performance-based compensation plans.

In public schools, some plans have lasted decades, but they have been transformed. Usually, what began as bonuses for better teaching or improved test scores morphed into extra pay for extra work, or spreading small payments across large numbers of teachers to gain greater participation and legitimacy. In Houston, for example, 80 percent of 12,000 teachers received a bonus in 2004—the maximum was $440. "It's not an incentive," the president of the teachers' union told a reporter. "It's almost a joke." Historically, paying teachers more for better teaching has, at best, a bleak record and, at worst, has failed.

Why has merit pay contained such lethal genes? The answers lie in two questions teachers ask, but which are often ignored by administrators and policymakers.

• Will the plan recognize that teaching differs from most other work?

• How come that teacher got a bonus and I didn't?

The first question underscores that teaching is different from ironing shirts, selling houses, or fastening chips to a motherboard. Teaching is not piecework. Most important, there is no checklist that objectively captures "good" teaching. (We place the word "good" in quotation marks to acknowledge that there are many forms of effective

Pay plans have a better chance at success when teachers have a say in the goals that are set and the measures used to judge teaching.

teaching, not just one.)

Consider why such a checklist is hard to compile. Teachers know that success with students depends upon their subject knowledge, skills, and awareness of students' background as displayed through classroom interactions. Teachers know that family background plays an important part in determining students' motivation and work behavior and what they learn. Finally, teachers know from experience that others (e.g., principals, parents, students, other teachers, taxpayers) have their own ideas of "good" teaching, including those officials who end up evaluating the quality of their teaching. All of these factors can influence what the teacher does after she closes the classroom door.

Although no single checklist recognizing all the factors influencing teaching and learning exists, most teachers would agree that the basic ingredients of effectiveness are well-prepared lessons, active engagement of students in those lessons through different teaching methods, monitoring of youngsters' academic progress, and managing their behavior. Who determines whether these essentials are being met is a question that teachers would ask regarding any merit-pay plan.

In their gut, teachers know teaching is not a cut-and-dried set of tasks, but a mix of evidenced-based practice, art, and intuitive judgments seasoned by a dash of luck. Anyone suggesting a sure-fire formula for "good" teaching would have a tough time convincing most teachers that such a recipe applies to them.

So the answer to the first question has to assure teachers that the merit-pay plan recognizes the imprecise, ambiguous, artistic, and interactive work that is teaching and other factors that shape student learning. In those places where merit-pay plans have failed most teachers were uninvolved in their design and ultimately unconvinced of their fairness, particularly after mediocre teachers were rewarded.

The second question—how come that teacher got a bonus and I didn't?—goes to the heart of the process whereby supervisors (usually principals) determine who has earned extra pay for better performance. If teachers known to be loafers receive bonuses, a merit-pay plan is doomed. If excellent teachers who have spoken out in faculty meetings or questioned administrators are denied bonuses, merit pay has little chance of gaining legitimacy among teachers. Unfortunately, merit-pay plans have yet to convince the very people they are supposed to motivate that the process is fair and untainted by personal favor.

The solution…in our view

If merit-pay plans are designed with little concern for teachers' sense of fairness and legitimacy, the lethal genes described above will guarantee an early death. However, that need not be the case every time compensation for performance is proposed. Many teachers yearn for a fair process of rewarding excellence in teaching and improved student learning. In one 2003 survey, 85 percent of teachers said that providing salary incentives would "help a lot" in retaining effective teachers.[49]

Teachers want plans that answer their questions and give serious consideration to the issues they raise about pay for performance. As top business, civic, educational, and philanthropic leaders who formed the Teaching Commission reported in "Teaching at Risk: A Call To Action" in 2004: "A performance-based evaluation needs … to be carefully designed and subject to checks and balances—including the involvement of teachers in the evaluation process—to prevent either favoritism or punishment of excellent teachers who 'rock the boat.' "[50]

Serious and sustained involvement of teachers at the very beginning of discussions about merit pay is a necessary (but not sufficient) condition. When teachers have a say in the goals that are set and the measures used to judge teaching performance and can choose from an array of opportunities (e.g., mentoring new teachers, developing curriculum and assessments, teaching demonstration lessons) to reach those agreed-upon goals, then that involvement lends a legitimacy to merit pay that has been missing in action for decades.

The Denver experience with ProComp, the Chattanooga plan of professional development and awarding bonuses to teachers who not only volunteer to teach in high-poverty schools but also raise students' test scores, and programs in a few other districts have taken seriously teacher involvement in merit-pay planning. Plans such as these promise positive outcomes for teachers, students, and the larger community.

Putting Mayors In Charge

More big-city mayors are taking control of school systems, putting their reputations and careers on the line. But the results of these changes in governance are decidedly mixed.

"If reading and math scores aren't significantly higher, I will look in the mirror and say I've failed." A reasonable guess as to who said this in 2002 would be a superintendent of schools. Actually, it was New York City Mayor Michael Bloomberg who then went on to say, "I have never failed at anything in my life." A few years earlier, Boston Mayor Tom Menino, standing on the steps of a high school denied accreditation, said to the city's voters: "I want to be judged as your mayor by what happens now in the Boston Public Schools. I expect you to hold me accountable…. If I fail, judge me harshly." [51]

New York City and Boston are not exceptions. Since the mid-1990s, Chicago, Cleveland, Philadelphia, and Detroit have seen their mayors deeply engaged in shaping the school district or actually appointing the superintendent. Other mayors in Washington, D.C.; Oakland, Calif.; and Hartford, Conn., who have had little direct influence on their cities' school boards have appointed more board members in an effort to shape school policies. Big-city mayors have, at best, an indirect influence on schools, much less classroom teaching. So, why are they betting their political futures on improving students' academic performance?

Where did the idea originate?

A century ago, good-government urban reformers changed their city charters to separate public schools from mayoral control. They were angered and sickened by the many mayors who had assembled political machines and appointed cronies to run city police, fire, sanitation, and other departments, including the schools. Mayors frequently appointed political hacks to school boards that then handed out teacher and principal jobs to machine supporters like turkeys at holiday time. Mayors looked upon schools, sanitation, police, and fire departments as employment bureaus. Reformers wanted independently elected school boards and a firewall between these boards and mayors to put schools out of the reach of city politics. By the 1920s, progressive reformers had succeeded in sealing off schools from mayoral influence by establishing non-partisan elected school boards and civil service exams to screen out unqualified job-seekers. Most cities (except for a few such as Chicago and Baltimore) elected mayors who kept their hands off boards of education.

In the decades following World War II, however, demography altered major cities. After four years of war, white middle-class families in cities wanted a patch of lawn, more space for their children to play, and larger homes in suburbs. Immigrants, the poor, and minorities swept into cities seeking cheap housing and jobs. Slums, crime, increasing racial conflict, and periodic unemployment accelerated the exodus of middle-class families and caused businesses and industry to move away from cities to places with lower taxes and less crime, thereby drawing taxable wealth and jobs from cities. Less tax revenue meant urban schools received less funding, even though the needs of low-income minority children for additional services in and out of schools escalated. Students' academic performance got worse; more high school students dropped out before graduating.

Although parents, business leaders, and civic elites looked toward schools as the linchpin to a city's economic success, many urban boards of education and their superintendents openly squabbled with one another, turning the school chief's job into a revolving door. School boards could not reverse the downward spiral of community poverty and crime, high dropout rates, and low academic achievement. In different cities, elected mayors, fearing impending economic disaster, intervened.

What problem is mayoral control intended to solve?

Since the 1970s, most urban school boards were impotent, with dismal records of one failed reform after another and zero accountability. Anxious to revive their cities economically and culturally, in the 1990s, business leaders, state officials, parents, and civic elites pushed for changes in city charters to give mayors responsibility for what happens in schools. When mayors take control of the school district, authority for governing schools generally shifts from non-partisan elected school boards to a Republican or Democratic city hall. The mayor or a mayoral-appointed board selects the superintendent. A mayor can now mobilize citywide campaigns to support schools. A mayor can bring more city resources (e.g., housing, employment, police, recreation, social services) to the table to help schools. And if a mayor fails, voters can boot him or her out of office.

In Chicago, Cleveland, Boston, and New York, mayors appoint both school boards and the schools' superintendent or chief executive officer (CEO). Boston voters, for example, passed a referendum in 1992 ending the elected school committee that had governed schools for decades and giving Mayor Menino the authority to appoint a school committee and superintendent. The prevailing belief among each city's civic and business leaders, that poor school performance was rooted in defective school board policies, led to the same solution: that a dramatic change in governance would reverse shabby academic performance.[52]

Does mayoral control work?

Some results of mayoral control are evident. Familiar conflicts between elected boards and their superintendents amplified in the media seldom occur when mayors appoint top school officials. In most cases, mayoral control of the school system has led to centralized decisionmaking by the superintendents and their deputies. Business and civic elites gain more influence over schools since newly appointed board members are often drawn from mayor-friendly groups. Schools now offer once-separate city services to patrons (e.g., community centers, child care, recreation, social services).

Yet at the same time, mayoral-appointed boards become more distant from constituents. No longer is there a monthly public forum to debate school policy.

But do these changes in governance improve academic performance, the primary reason for the reform? The evidence, at best, is mixed. Over the past few years in some mayoral-control cities (New York, Boston, Chicago, Cleveland), elementary school test scores have seen modest increases, but secondary schools have registered hardly any change. And, in Detroit, test scores have fallen across the board. Gaps in test scores between white and minority students have narrowed in some places where mayors control schools, yet widened in others. There is no pattern of school success that can be attributed to shifting policymaking responsibility from elected school boards to mayors.[53]

Two reasons might explain the absence of any pattern. First, there are no recipes for improving test scores that mayors can hand competent educators to pursue. Appointing an outside superstar superintendent, business executive, or corporate lawyer is, at best, a mere beginning. To improve teaching and learning requires connecting the many links, from the mayor to his or her appointed school board, the superintendent, headquarters officials, school principals, teachers, and, ultimately, the students. It takes hard work and ample resources invested in schools, a stable and experienced teaching staff, and sustained support for teachers and principals. Simply ordering educators to do better makes catchy newspaper headlines—New York Mayor Bloomberg said "there is a direct link from the teacher's desk in the classroom, right to the mayor's desk in City Hall"—but no mayor's influence reaches a teacher after she closes the classroom door. So moving political control from an elected school board to the mayor shifts power to hire and fire superintendents, but does not necessarily make much difference in running schools or teaching students.[54]

Second, a mayor's time for schools is limited by competing electoral concerns over poverty, homelessness, the tax base, crime, and public health, to mention only a few issues. Because school improvement takes far more time—anywhere from five to 10 years—than the common four-year electoral cycle for which mayors campaign, mayors must present the best possible case that they have succeeded. That is hard to do with the schools that need lots of time and help to succeed. Note further that when a mayor leaves office, the educational agenda may well shift. For these reasons, governance change may be popular, but it is severely limited in its ability to alter classroom practice and improve students' academic performance. "Taking over a school system," Columbus, Ohio, Mayor Michael Coleman said in 2003, "is not synonymous with an improved school system." [55]

The solution…in our view

Mayoral control may work in some cities and not others. Boston voters abolished their elected school board because it failed to improve schools and its conflicts with superintendents became a chronic embarrassment. Voters wanted mayoral control over the schools. San Diego, to cite a counter-example, has a city-manager system of local governance, and the mayor and city manager have largely avoided the turmoil that has plagued that district's schools since 1998.

Simply put, governance change in and of itself does not necessarily make better schools.

In cities such as Washington, D.C., and Pittsburgh, elected school boards have lost their way in trying to improve schools, yet other urban elected school boards have succeeded in slowly improving their schools. Seattle, San Diego, Cincinnati, Minneapolis, Denver, Sacramento (Calif.), and many other urban districts wrestling with lack of resources, poor neighborhoods, teacher mobility, and other serious issues have used traditional governance to work toward school improvement. These school boards hired superintendents who have held administrators accountable for student performance, expanded preschools, built instructional support systems for teachers and principals, and reported steady gains in elementary school scores (but not secondary schools). These school boards recognized that sustained support for change is an essential condition as they press forward in secondary schools recruiting qualified teachers, establishing small high schools, and focusing on instructional improvement. In short, nothing miraculous resides in mayoral control, traditional school board governance, or hybrids of each. What matters is local context, leadership, and political will.

Ordering educators to do better makes for catchy headlines but no mayor's influence reaches a teacher after she closes the classroom door.

Giving Schools More Control

A strategy that keeps coming back,
school-based management can be effective,
but it takes a clear purpose, investment in training,
and long-term commitment to work.

To make schools better, turn decisions over to those closest to the schools. A reaction against top-down, one-size-fits-all policymaking by districts and states, the goal of school-based management is to improve teaching and learning by getting the principal, teachers, parents, and even students in the higher grades involved in decisions about their schools. Since each school is different, those most directly affected by certain key choices should be the ones to make them. So the argument goes.

School-based management (SBM) appears under different names (site-based budgeting, school-based decisionmaking) and takes many different forms. The basic idea is that each school controls its own budget and that choices about spending are made by a group of school and community representatives. In some cases, this group or council is made up of teachers and the principal; in others, parents and community members and students are included. In some cases, educators outnumber or equal non-educators; in others, it is the opposite.[56] Under some versions of SBM councils share power with the principal; in others, they are advisory only. Some can hire or fire the principal; others can do neither or both.

In theory, school councils can decide everything from the school schedule to who is hired and what is taught. In practice, SBM operates under many constraints that curtail total freedom. Some of these restrictions are tied to funding. For example, federal grants under the No Child Left Behind Act (including Title I) come with many strings attached. Even state and district general funds—those not earmarked for specific expenses—are not really up for grabs. Busing schedules dictate when school starts and finishes each day; state laws often set requirements for instructional time and courses; union contracts and state laws limit who can be hired and fired.

School-based management comes and goes like the wind. Every decade or so many school districts, especially large ones, move from highly centralized systems to decentralized systems. Then they go back in the other direction. Take the case of Chicago. In 1988, a new state law required Chicago to decentralize by establishing local community-run boards to hire principals and manage each school. Less than a decade later, revisions of the state law placed control of the schools in the hands of the mayor who concentrated power back at the top of the system. In 2005, another turn-around was reported in the *Chicago Tribune* as if decentralizing had never happened before:

"Chicago school officials plan to take a first step toward decentralizing the massive system next month when they give 85 [out of 600] of the best-run schools sweeping autonomy in teaching students, training educators and spending money. The decision . . . is part of a long-term vision of untangling an entrenched bureaucracy long viewed as one of the most formidable barriers to school reform."[57]

Chicago's story points to the different reasons put forth for SBM. One is the belief that democratic participation should be the cornerstone of public schools and therefore local communities should be the engine of school reform. Another is the belief that district central offices are administrative nightmares that do much to get in the way of school improvement and little to help. Yet another is the idea that control over the budget is a reward to schools that have already demonstrated their success.

Where did SBM originate?

School-based management dates from the earliest days of public schooling in America, when schools were run by individual boards of trustees. The ultimate in local control, these boards wielded considerable power, and members sometimes outnumbered teachers.[58] They were not subject to state or federal control. To some, these represent the glory days of democratic participation; to others, differences among schools due to their wealth or poverty were inherently unfair.[59]

As the country became more urbanized in the early 20th century, states slowly consolidated hundreds of thousands of mostly one-school districts into nearly 15,000 districts by the 1980s. In the largest of these, layers of bureaucracy and regulation greatly restrict what individual schools can decide to do on their own. Even in small districts the many state and federal programs, each with its own set of regulations and staff to make sure they are followed, make management cumbersome at best.

In response to the growing number of district staff and their control over what schools could and could not do, urban districts became the whipping boy for the problems of public education. Critics judged central office staffs inefficient, undemocratic, and ineffective and called for downsizing: Let the schools manage themselves and rely on the district only for the essentials like transportation, meals, and facilities.

Spurred by restructuring of large businesses in the 1970s and '80s, together with studies of Japanese management that championed delegating power to workers, school-based management took off. By 1990, more than a third of the nation's public schools had some form of school-based management. Virtually every large urban system has now been through at least one cycle of centralization to SBM and back.

What problem is SBM intended to solve?

Rationales for implementing SBM and the claims for what it will accomplish cover broad territory.

In some cases, school-based management is put forth as a solution to inefficient, rule-bound, and even corrupt district central offices and local boards. Instead of dictating what schools should do from above, reformers believe that teachers, parents, and principals should be the ones deciding what their schools should look like. In other cases, it is simply a matter of delegating the budget to the school without any expectations about who—beyond the principal—should be involved in making decisions.

SBM is also promoted as a way to put more authority in the hands of teachers who, proponents argue, know their students best. This view emphasizes empowering professionals rather than bureaucrats.

Advocates claim it will increase student achievement, or at least set the stage for such increases. In some cases, SBM can also be viewed as an end in itself—a mechanism for increasing participation in school decisions. Especially when educators and community members view local boards of education with distrust (or anger), simply increasing democratic participation at the school level is a valued goal.

As the earlier Chicago story illustrates, SBM can play another role: a reward for success. In this scenario, the idea is that schools "earn" the right to be freed from rules that dictate what they should do. This idea is consistent with the current emphasis on standards and test scores, which leads districts to mandate particular solutions to counteract low test scores. If a school scores low, for whatever reason, it must follow the district's prescribed program. If it scores high, it is granted the freedom to design its own programs.

Does school-based management work?

Whatever the rationale, SBM typically boils down to electing a group of people for a year or two to work together to improve their school. In practice, such groups spend time deciding how they will operate, setting up committees, and developing a school improvement plan based on test scores and other information. By the next year, however, new test scores arrive and the group—with new members—revises the plan. Translating plans into action proves elusive.

School-based management involves many pieces, including legal authority to run schools, who sits on the school council, the size of the budget they control, and what decisions are up for grabs. Whether it works, therefore, can mean many different things. For example, did it happen? Did schools actually get control over their budgets? Oftentimes, this is the first stumbling block. Delegation of power in practice is usually far less than advertised. One study of SBM in large school systems found that the percent of the budget delegated to schools ranged from about 6 percent to almost 80 percent.[60]

Not surprisingly, even when schools have some significant control over how to spend the budget, school councils tend to make changes only on the margins. Partly, this is because major decisions about curriculum and testing have already been made by the district or state. But it is also because council members and their constituencies know and care about issues of discipline, facilities, and extracurricular activities, rather than classroom teaching. When councils do turn to matters of

School-based management involves many pieces, including legal authority to run schools, who sits on the school council, the size of the budget they control, and what decisions are up for grabs.

instruction, their options are limited. For example, if test scores declined in math, council members might recommend devoting a few more minutes to math each day.

Does SBM cause test scores to go up? Certainly not by itself. And why should it? Imagine bringing together a group of teachers and parents who have never worked together—and may well have never been part of a decisionmaking group. Now, add the principal, the person responsible for evaluating the teachers. One can imagine a number of benefits from such an enterprise, such as better communication between teachers and parents and among teachers about issues facing the school. But tracing a direct line from such a group to higher test scores is much more problematic. As the superintendent of the highly touted Edmonton, Canada, school-based model put it in 2005: "There are some sensible things that districts can do, and I think site-based [SBM] has a lot of power. But I think even its authors would tell you it's not a solution to raising achievement results."[61] The Edmonton schools instead have focused on measures of parent, community, staff, and student satisfaction as gauged by annual surveys.

No research studies have found strong and lasting links between SBM and test scores. For test scores to go up, teachers and students must change what they do in classrooms. A school-based council can certainly be a starting place. It is difficult to make a convincing case that those outside the school could do a better job of deciding, for even if they have more knowledge and better ideas, it is still those in the school who have to make them work.

However, SBM is not risk-free. Mandating shared decisionmaking with little control over the budget leads to bickering and frustration. Delegating budgetary authority to an authoritarian principal alienates staff and community. Even when these problems are absent, schools with the most enterprising leadership are best able to take advantage of budgetary control. A study of Cleveland's SBM experience found that those who already knew how to work the system were able to accomplish the most.[62]

The solution…in our view

For school-based management to work, it takes a clear purpose and a long-term commitment. It requires real control over decisions, which translates into control over a large portion of the school budget. It also requires an investment in training so those involved understand their roles and options. Without these pieces, SBM can easily become an empty and time-consuming process of meetings and plan-writing.

SBM has the potential to empower those closest to the students to design educational programs tailored to their needs. On the other hand, such design requires technical know-how, which might not be well-represented in some school communities. Making SBM work well also necessitates a system that allocates funds fairly and a decisionmaking structure that fits the school.

Creating systems to allocate and track budgets and to train those who are expected to make wise decisions takes considerable time and patience, both to create effective systems and to get teachers, administrators, and communities on board. Finding the right balance between district or state direction and school flexibility also takes time and patience.

Begun as a pilot 30 years ago, the biggest lesson of the Edmonton SBM experience might be the importance of sticking with an idea and at the same time adapting it.[63] The notion that a state or district in the United States would stand by an education reform for 30 years boggles the mind, yet a large chunk of time is precisely what SBM will need as a necessary (but not sufficient) condition to work.

Reforming How Schools Are Organized

In this section, we focus on the keystone organization in K-12 education: the age-graded school. Developed in the mid-19th century to remedy the inefficiencies of one-room schoolhouses, the age-graded school—6-year-olds in 1st grade, and so on—remains the norm. And, while the system reforms described in the previous section turn on changes in the ways schools are organized, reform proposals generally view the age-graded school as a given.

The reforms discussed in this section address how grades are configured (moving to K-8 schools), the size of classes (reducing class size), and whether to hold back failing students (ending social promotion). Similarly, we address borrowing good ideas from other schools (best practices) and changing schedules during the day or year (extending time in school), as well as eliminating ability-grouping and reforming high schools.

Research-Based Best Practices

Hoping to learn from others' examples, schools and educators are turning to studies that examine what the most successful schools are doing well and what strategies can be duplicated elsewhere.

"Best practices" exist in every field, from corporate management to NASCAR. In fact, there are thousands, if not hundreds of thousands, of "best practices" in every profession, if searches on the Internet are any indication. The idea is simple and compelling. Some corporations are more profitable than others, some racetracks are safer than others, some schools score higher than others. So, it makes sense that organizations that are not doing as well might look to others and ask, what are they doing to get better results?

The desire to learn from others has produced a raft of studies of best practices in education. From the "unusually effective" schools of the 1970s to the "beating the odds" schools of the early 2000s, these studies identify schools with poor and minority students that perform better than expected, and seek to identify the practices that led to these results.

Today's "best practices," deduced from observations of schools with increasing test scores and decreasing achievement gaps, fill the craving for specific suggestions to improve test scores that accountability pressures have generated. For a school or district looking to improve, the challenge is to figure out what conditions in the best-practice site enabled a practice to flourish and whether the struggling site has those conditions. Are the students similar? Is it the practices themselves or the skills of the people using them

that makes the difference in student achievement? How much teacher professional development was available? What other pieces have to be in place?

Here's an example. A "best practice" that appears on several such lists is frequent monitoring of student performance. Where this is done well, however, many other elements are in place. For example, a school that monitors student performance successfully is likely to be in a district that has created assessments to measure progress that can be used frequently, provided extensive training to teachers, and established an easy-to-use data system so that teachers can enter and retrieve data on individual students as needed. If a school simply adopts a new test for monitoring students without the other pieces, it will likely fail to produce the desired results. Even with all these pieces in place, the question remains of whether teachers have the knowledge to act on what they learn from the assessments.

Under time pressure to improve, educators often embrace practices reputed to be "best" that appear to meet their needs, without figuring out whether the necessary conditions are in place.

Where did the idea originate?

In 1966, the federally commissioned Coleman Report made a big splash. Its conclusion—that a student's family background has a bigger impact on academic achievement than school quality—

was often taken to mean that schools cannot make a difference. One response was to demonstrate that some schools clearly do.

In the early 1970s, a handful of researchers began looking at urban schools where students were performing above national norms. Building on this work, researcher Ronald Edmonds identified additional schools where poor children had higher test scores than expected given their backgrounds. He compiled a list of practices these "effective schools" had in common and launched a movement to help other schools establish these practices. Edmonds' five factors have been expanded and amended, but the essence of each one remains on almost every list of best practices: strong principal leadership, a pervasive instructional focus, orderly and safe climate, high expectations for students, and continuous assessment of student achievement.[1]

Edmonds and his successors rested their work on the presumption that if some children from poor families can succeed, all can. If some teachers repeatedly produce large achievement gains with poor children, all can. If some schools with mostly poor children repeatedly produce high test scores, all can. Although these claims seem hard to believe, the underlying motive is compelling: the belief that schools can improve, and that poverty and race are not excuses for providing substandard education. Hence, the hunt for schools and districts that can serve as proof that it is possible.

The idea of looking at exemplars to figure out what works got a second wind in the 1980s when Tom Peters and other observers of successful corporations spread the lingo of benchmarking and best practices in their writing.[2] The standards movement's banner, "all children can learn," and the requirement of the federal No Child Left Behind Act that all subgroups of students meet certain test score targets each year boosted motivation to find successful practices. As attention has shifted in recent years to the role of the school district, "best practices" research has turned attention to what districts do as well as individual schools.

Study after study has generated descriptions of practices found in schools with unusually high test scores. Some provide lists of practices while others have fuller descriptions and back them up with detailed case studies of individual schools and districts that give a sense of their history and how the practices fit together.

Most descriptions of best practices converge on a set of factors not unlike those originally identified by Ronald Edmonds. Although the broad brush strokes remain the same, the specific practices shift over time, as reform trends change in emphasis. In the early 1980s, for example, one "best practice" for districts, under the umbrella of school-based management, was to delegate decisions about curriculum and some other matters to individual schools. Today, it is a "best practice" for districts to use a single districtwide curriculum for all schools.

Although "best practices" seem to go hand in hand with high test scores, the research provides no guarantee that the practices themselves caused higher scores. Hence the importance of understanding the broader set of conditions that contributed to higher scores.

What problem is identifying "best practices" intended to solve?

The idea of identifying the practices of successful schools and districts is that others who are less successful can learn how to improve. But the problems that need solving are not simple ones.

Districts and schools do not purposely choose ineffective practices. Most aim to do well by their students. So, why are some less successful than others? Perhaps the real problem lies in understanding the answer to this question; that is, what are we doing wrong here? Different answers may suggest different courses of action.

Some "best practices" are self-evident. Kati Haycock of the Education Trust points to funding gaps between districts with the most and the fewest poor children, as well as gaps in the quality

Best practices are not magic bullets. Some success stories rely on exceptional people or circumstances, such as a school whose teachers and students have chosen to be there.

of teachers and curriculum between the poorest and the least-poor students.[3] Here the problem is not one of ignorance about what would help close the achievement gap; the problem is how to reduce gaps in funding and teacher and curriculum quality.

Other kinds of problems are more amenable to "best practices" research. Say a school or district has just adopted a new reading program. If a similar district adopted the same program a few years earlier and found it effective, what steps did it take? For example, what kind of training did teachers get, what problems did they encounter, how did they solve them? In short, how did they create the conditions for the "best practice" to work?

Do "best practices" work?

Well-documented practices from similar schools that have performed well year after year can provide a starting point for educators working to improve their schools. Reading about, and especially talking to, those involved at successful sites can be inspiring and open the door to new ways of thinking and new strategies. But the limitations need to be clear from the outset to avoid false promises.

Best practices are not magic bullets. Some success stories rely on exceptional people or circumstances, such as a school whose teachers

and students have chosen to be there. What works in these circumstances is unlikely to work elsewhere.

Other "best practices" are a flash in the pan, successful only for a brief time, or perhaps for a somewhat longer sizzle. But a change in principal or test or district mandates, or simply the passage of time, changes the results. The high turnover rate of teachers and principals in urban schools makes sustained efforts difficult. Even the excellent companies identified in the bestseller *In Search of Excellence* were no longer excellent a few years later. Many went downhill; some even folded.[4]

Studies identifying schools that outperform other schools with similar student bodies leave many questions unanswered. One is whether test scores, especially an average score based on one year, really indicate effectiveness. A school can have high scores in 3rd grade math and low scores in 3rd grade reading one year, and the reverse a year later. Or high scores in all subjects in one 3rd grade class and not the other. Or high scores in 3rd grade and low scores in 4th grade. On average, one school might appear to be "better" than another, but it may only be a few exceptional teachers—or a few exceptional students—who account for this difference. In other cases, the unmeasured characteristics of students (e.g., many are technically poor, but only because their parents are graduate students at Harvard) and the presence of unusual circumstances lead to questionable claims of success.[5]

Another unanswered question about best practices is just how they lead to higher-than-expected student achievement. Studies typically inquire about best practices and describe what is going on in the schools and districts that produce higher-than-expected test scores. But they are not able to link the practices directly to the results. So, for example, many studies conclude that instructional leadership is a best practice and may go further to describe the specific things an instructional leader does. But this list of behaviors is still many steps removed from what a teacher, principal, or superintendent actually needs to do to raise student test scores.

Practices that work well in one school may not fit in another. Their success inevitably depends upon a particular combination of interconnected practices, the skills and knowledge of the people using them, the school's history of innovation, and the conditions likely to support changes in their school.

Transplanting practices is akin to transplanting a tree. Unless the soil conditions are appropriate, the tree is unlikely to survive.

Even knowing the whole story behind a successful school does not tell others how to duplicate its winning ways. The essence of good practice is what goes on between a teacher and a student in a particular lesson. Program developers and education reformers would be out of business if this could be boiled down to a set of easy-to-follow steps.

The solution…in our view

Models of good practice are critical. They demonstrate what is possible. They suggest what the ingredients of success are. Whether the practices are those of an excellent teacher, an inspired principal, or a district's system for recruiting top educators, those who can observe good practice for an extended time begin to see how all the pieces fit together. But opportunities are rare for extended firsthand observation among education practitioners. Moreover, the distance between observing practice and duplicating it schoolwide, much less across a district, is huge. So it is not surprising that success on a small scale rarely becomes widespread. Most successes depend on too many specific conditions that often remain unidentified or cannot be replicated.

Many of the frameworks developed in the process of documenting successful schools and districts provide useful guides for educators to analyze their own organizations. The more that studies of best practices emphasize how and why certain results occur, the more useful they will be to educators. The more such studies provide

models of how educators can ask good questions about why their school or district is ineffective with some or all students, the more likely it is that educators will develop solutions that match their schools or districts.

Best practices cannot be easily transplanted, but the process of thinking through the problems they are intended to solve can lead to better solutions. In fact, this process can rightly shift the emphasis from transplanting one or two trees to improving the soil.

Ending Social Promotion

It seems illogical to pass students along when they are clearly not yet ready for the next grade, but difficult questions remain about the best way to identify and help children who aren't keeping up.

Lester finishes 3rd grade still struggling to read sentences without stumbling over several words. He doesn't like to read, but he does enjoy addition and subtraction, although again he works slowly and does not yet understand multiplication. His test scores on a typical timed standardized test are well below the 50th percentile—the national average. Still, he listens to the teacher and does his work. Should Lester advance to the 4th grade?

"No more social promotion!" has become a reform rallying cry, particularly in large urban districts faced with thousands of struggling students like Lester. Social promotion, in everyday language, means advancing students to the next grade despite evidence that they have not successfully met the school's criteria for their current grade.

Who could disagree with ending this seemingly illogical practice? A student who doesn't have the knowledge and skills to succeed in 3rd grade will surely not be able to succeed in 4th grade. And the 4th grade teacher will face students unprepared to tackle 4th grade work.

If ending social promotion makes so much sense, why not do it everywhere?

But a closer look raises some tough questions: How are "passing" and "failing" determined? What happens to students who are held back? Do better alternatives than social promotion exist to help students who fall behind?

Where did the idea originate?

Social promotion happens because our system of schools is "age graded." This means that students move through school according to age. When you are 6, you are in 1st grade, 7 in 2nd grade, and so on. The United States borrowed this idea from Prussia in the mid-19th century. In the late 19th century, however, most American students left school by the 4th or 5th grade and went to work. Only a handful ever attended high school. Reformers in the early 20th century introduced kindergarten to bring students into public school earlier and junior high schools to keep them there longer. They pushed through compulsory school attendance laws and legislation prohibiting child labor. By the 1930s, influenced by the Great Depression, millions of students were staying in school longer, and nearly half of all students were receiving high school diplomas.

As public schooling through high school became common, however, school boards and superintendents faced a new problem. Many students couldn't keep up and were held back, but retaining large numbers of students meant that too many older students congregated in the lower grades.

As a result, in the 1930s, educators came up with the idea of social promotion as a solution to the "pileup" problem. Most school boards defined "passing" a grade by the number of failures the organization could tolerate—usually less than 5 percent of the students in a grade. Since students are expected to move up a grade each year, formal or informal policies usually define passing in a way that ends up promoting most students. And that's what has happened in public schools today. Most students are moved to the next grade, ready or not, leaving room for the incoming class of students.

Of course, school boards in the 1930s and 1940s could have spent lots of money helping students catch up with their age-mates. Or, administrators could have intervened in the early grades when academic troubles first surfaced. Both would have reduced social promotions considerably, but, at the time, the money simply wasn't there. When money did become available in later years, summer school emerged as the second-chance option for failing students.

What problem is banning social promotion intended to solve?

Banning social promotion is supposed to end the practice of pushing students through school when they are not yet equipped to learn at a higher level. It's a problem with serious consequences for individual students who fail to learn and at the institutional level for schools and universities, as well as for employers who must teach such students what they have missed. When students graduate from high school without knowing how to read or write, politicians blame social promotion.

In today's high-stakes-accountability climate, ending social promotion is also intended to motivate students to work harder. The argument is that, if students know they will not move to the next grade unless they pass a test, they will be inspired to work harder to avoid being held back. As a result, more students will earn a passing grade, and the number retained will be smaller. For those who do not pass the test, second chances are often available in summer school.

Under the current wave of standards-based reform, a ban on social promotion implicitly tackles a perennial problem faced by teachers: how to decide whether to promote particular students. Educators worry about which factors to weigh and the best balance among such things as grades, test scores, and

behavior. Should the teachers promote an elementary school student who reads well, but is failing math? Or a student who has made substantial progress but started school far behind his peers? Or a student who is well-behaved and works hard but makes little progress?

Today, if a teacher's district prohibits social promotion, he may have little or no voice in deciding whether a child is ready for the next grade. Prodded by the federal No Child Left Behind Act, most urban districts are turning to test scores as the primary, if not sole, criterion for passing. This may make the decision simpler for the teacher, but less appropriate for the student whose particular strengths and needs are no longer taken into account.

There is also the problem of setting the test score that will define promotion or retention. There is no guarantee that a test-based standard will keep the number of failures relatively small, particularly if the cutoff score is tied to national averages. In Chicago, the policy begun in 1996 to end social promotion resulted in *one-third* of the students failing to make the test score cutoffs. Fortunately, summer school provided a second chance for many of the students, especially those from higher-performing schools.[6]

Does banning social promotion work?

Students have always been held back. Today, many students, averaging 13 percent overall and as high as 50 percent for black males, are retained, and rates have increased since 1970.[7] Yet, research on retention has turned up few positive results for individual students. These youngsters are more likely to continue their record of poor achievement and more likely to drop out of school than their peers who have been promoted.[8] In fact, retention turns out to be the strongest predictor for dropping out of school.[9]

Research in Chicago indicates that most students at risk of being held back based on a standardized test score are initially motivated to attend summer school to increase their test scores. However, this finding does not hold true for the lowest-scoring students. And, even for those able to raise their test scores, a

No single solution will solve all the dilemmas posed by students who fall behind their peers. But for most students emphasizing early intervention and providing second chances is critical.

year later they continue to perform poorly.[10]

In general, students who do not pass a grade the first time around are unlikely to do much better the second time around, all else being equal (which it usually is). So unless cutoff scores are lowered, students will begin to "pile up" in the lower grades. Worse yet, for those students who repeat a grade twice, chances of dropping out of school soar.[11]

But the real problem is that low-performing students do not benefit either from being passed to the next grade or from being retained in their current grade. For many low-performing students—but not the lowest-performing—summer school focused on test preparation can indeed raise test scores in the short run. But no research demonstrates that this immediate payoff has any lasting effect. Whether or not they are retained, these students continue to perform poorly on schoolwork and tests.[12]

The fact is that banning social promotion freezes the already rigid time frame built into the traditional age-graded system for low-performing students.

The solution…in our view

Reformers who introduced the idea of standards-based reform talked about the fact that most students could reach the bar, *but some would take more time than others.* They anticipated that linking high standards to an age-graded system would snare low-performing students. In some cases, that has happened.

But the solution to so-called social promotion is neither to pass students to the next grade if they are unprepared nor to hold them back for more of the same. Besides making sure students are as prepared as possible when they begin school, the answer lies in making careful judgments of whether individual students are ready to move to the next level. This, in turn, means figuring out ways to break out of the straitjacket of age-graded schooling that requires everyone to progress at the same rate.

Several approaches are possible, each with significant drawbacks. *All* are needed if low-performing students are to have real chances to succeed.

One approach is to reorganize students by skill level for each subject and move them ahead as they master skills. This results in ungraded classes—that is, classes with students of mixed ages. Nine-year-old Lester might find himself with a group of 9- to 11-year-olds for math, and he might be grouped with younger students for reading, not his best subject. The drawback is resistance from parents and teachers accustomed to an age-graded school.

Another approach is to identify students with academic problems earlier and to intervene through tutoring and extra instructional time after school, on Saturdays, and during the summer. The challenge lies in hiring and training more teachers and encouraging parents to see that their children attend.

Yet another partial solution is to provide more and better instruction during the regular school day to students at risk of failure. Here the drawback is that the lowest-performing students are unlikely to be assigned the best teachers. And time during the school day for extra instruction is limited.

No single solution will solve all the dilemmas posed by students who fall behind their peers. But for most students, emphasizing prevention of failure in the first place, and providing early intervention and second chances through extra study time is fundamental. As standards are raised, the quality and prevalence of early intervention and second chances needs to increase. Simply holding students back—or passing them after intensive test preparation—is not a solution. More time and better instruction is.

To Track or Not To Track

The standards movement and its call for all students to achieve has added new pressure to end the practice of tracking, or separating students according to their academic abilities.

At Columbia High School in Maplewood, N.J., most of the students are black, although in advanced classes white students make up the vast majority. In lower math classes blacks significantly outnumber whites. As one senior put it: "You can tell right away, just by looking into a classroom, what level it is." While the high school boasts of its racial diversity, collegelike campus, top scholars, great sports teams, and alumni celebrities, racially segregated classes have prompted protests from its black student leaders. Columbia High, like many other high schools with mixed racial and ethnic populations, strives to celebrate cultural diversity and to encourage high academic achievement through tracking.[13]

Tracking (or leveling) means grouping students by ability or past performance in middle and high school subjects—sometimes called "homogeneous grouping" by educators. The theory behind tracking is that creating classes (e.g., Advanced Placement Biology, Basic Math) that decrease the disparities in students' capacities increases the chances teachers can provide instruction tailored to different groups. Tracking assumes that teachers can be patient with low achievers while pushing high achievers. High-performing students benefit by not waiting for others to catch up with them. As one champion of gifted classes asked: "Do we improve the skills of our Olympic swimmers by asking that they take time to teach non-swimmers

how to swim?" Furthermore, low-performing students benefit by not having to compete against high achievers.[14]

The argument against tracking is that ability groups for top achievers create academic elites and segregate students by race, social class, and ethnicity, thereby depriving low-performing students of peers they can emulate. Moreover, critics argue that grouping low-performing students in separate classes (particularly if they are mostly minority) signals to teachers to lower their academic expectations and deliver an inferior quality of content and skills. As one white student at Columbia High School in a lower-level, predominantly black math class said about the teacher's low expectations: "It makes you feel like you're in a hole."

Debates over district decisions to launch, cut back, or end tracking have broken out repeatedly across the country, not just at Columbia High School. Parents of special needs children, for example, have pressed to "mainstream" their children since the mid-1970s rather than keep them in separate classrooms. Parents of minority students who have been refused entry into Advanced Placement or honors classes have protested. Researchers have questioned the benefits of leveling and tracking practices.

Current reform efforts to provide a rigorous high school curriculum to all students and the No Child Left Behind Act's requirement that all students reach proficiency in reading, math, and other subjects by 2014 add pressure to "de-track" schools, for how else can all parents be assured that their children have access to what they need to succeed?

Where did the idea of tracking originate?

Even though educators largely accepted tracking as a worthwhile tool over the past century, they have debated its effectiveness time and again. After the civil rights movement, court cases, and research studies since the 1960s, however, the debate spilled outside the education community. Since the 1970s, many policymakers, parents, teachers, and researchers have raised serious questions about the accuracy of the tests used to place students in groups, particularly for minority and poor children. They have also questioned the quality of teaching and learning delivered in lower-track classes, and the overall worth of ability grouping itself. These debates reflected a social fact: American schools are not only about teaching and learning; they are also virtual ladders to good-paying jobs, higher social status, and a better life. For champions of tracking, sorting students by performance offers a firm grip on one rung of the ladder.

Research documenting the shortcomings of tracking in secondary schools gained widespread support in the late 1980s. Researchers found that higher percentages of low-income minorities were assigned to lower-level classes than middle- and upper-middle-income whites. Those lower-level classes were often taught by less-qualified teachers, and the content offered in these classrooms differed from what was taught to upper-level students. As one researcher said in 1985: "No group of students has been found to benefit consistently from being in a homogenous group."[15]

By the early 1990s, the National Governors Association, the National Education Association, the National Council of English Teachers, and the California Department of Education recommended that tracking be abolished. Some districts ended tracking in their middle and high schools.[16]

What problem is de-tracking intended to solve?

Sorting students by performance and ability, particularly when that sorting results in large numbers of poor and minority students in low-tracked classes, can amount to a resegregation of students within a school. According to many researchers, policymakers, and practitioners, this segregation is psychologically, educationally, and organizationally harmful to all students in that school. Thus, abolishing tracks in both middle and high schools, and ensuring that all students are in mixed-ability groups, helps students learn from one another in more democratic settings.

Does de-tracking work?

Before answering the question of whether de-tracking works, it is important to determine to what degree tracking has been abolished. In Massachusetts and California, state officials have mandated de-tracking in middle schools. Districts across the country have adopted the reform, according to reports by researchers and school boards. Yet in 1993, researchers found that 86 percent of high schools offered courses in which students were grouped by ability or past performance (90 percent in math and 72 percent in English). In 2000, of all public high schools in Maryland, 67 percent reported using tracking in four academic subjects. So, while the reform of de-tracking has occurred in some places, tracking remains the dominant practice of organizing instruction in many secondary schools.[17]

And what does the research say about de-tracking? Some studies tout the many benefits that flow from mixing students together both for the gifted and lowest-performing students. Students who ordinarily would have been excluded from Advanced Placement courses, for example, were allowed to take the subject and did well on exams. Other studies challenge these findings.

At this time, no researcher, policymaker, or public official can prove whether tracking or de-tracking yields better results in raising academic achievement, getting kids into college, or boosting self-esteem for all students, some, or none at all. Most studies, however, do not assess whether social benefits exist from mixing students of different performance levels and cultural backgrounds, especially since the work world that these students will soon enter does not engage in tracking.[18]

The solution...in our view

If research does not settle the question of whether de-tracking works for the most able, least able, and disabled, what is the solution for tracking's negative consequences? The standards, testing, and accountability movement intends for every student—including disabled and non-English-speaking students—to be, in the language of No Child Left Behind, "academically proficient" by 2014. And, most parents want their sons and daughters to enter college. In the midst of these high expectations for schools, practices that track students in high school subjects (e.g., AP biology) remain.

One solution is to allow all students to enroll in academically rigorous classes while providing the extra help some need to succeed. Structured study groups and tutoring have strong track records as effective ways to provide such help. Similarly, gathering students in need of special help or enrichment at certain times and disbanding such groups when the work is completed seems sensible. But excluding highly motivated, lower-performing students from Advanced Placement or International Baccalaureate courses smacks of unfairness. The challenge lies in balancing the values of equity and achievement at Columbia High and thousands of other high schools.

Another solution is to make certain that 7th and 8th grade students, their parents, and their counselors fully understand what is required for different college and career paths. Too often, students are locked into a track of coursework in 8th grade that guarantees they will not be prepared for college by their senior year. Many students are totally unaware of this fact.

De-tracking has clearly challenged educators' and parents' assumptions that some students can't hack tough academic subjects by showing that they can, given the opportunity and support. The challenge now is to provide students with the options and the help they need to succeed.

Rethinking High School

Business and policy elites are focusing on high schools as troubled institutions, proposing breaking many down into smaller schools and boosting academic rigor overall.

" **A**merica's high schools are obsolete. ...I am terrified for our workforce," Microsoft Chairman Bill Gates told the governors and business leaders who assembled in 2005 to create an agenda for improving high schools.[19] At the National Education Summit, high schools were cast as the core education problem facing the country, "the front line in the battle for America's future economic prosperity."[20]

Changes in the global and U.S. economy place new pressures on our high schools. Political and business leaders point to U.S. slippage in international rankings of high school and college graduation rates; goals of citizenship and building character are rarely mentioned. As jobs are outsourced to countries where labor is cheaper and workers more motivated, the pressure to increase the academic rigor and the graduation rate of high schools has intensified.

The number of students who are leaving school before graduation is on the rise. Having peaked at close to 80 percent in 1969, the overall U.S. high school graduation rate has dropped over the past decade and is now closer to 70 percent.[21] This means that only seven out of 10 students who start high school finish, and half of those are not prepared for college-level work. Of the seven who graduate, four continue their education and just two finish college on time.[22] For students who are black, Hispanic, or poor, the statistics are much

worse. According to the Manhattan Institute, a think tank based in New York City, only half of black and Hispanic students finish high school, and most of those are not eligible for college admission: only 20 percent of Hispanic students and 23 percent of black students are college-ready compared with 40 percent of white students.[23] For youths who are not college-bound, the options are dismal. Often, only dumbed-down, dead-end jobs remain, even for those with a high school diploma.

One response to this situation, fueled by substantial investments from the Bill & Melinda Gates Foundation, is to create small, rigorous high schools. The idea is that small high schools—those with fewer than 400 students or roughly 100 per grade level—provide a more personalized and safer environment than the much larger 2,000- to 4,000-student high schools in the biggest cities. Reformers believe that small high schools will encourage more students to stay in school and to graduate ready for college. And, they assert, increasing the academic rigor of coursework will produce more graduates ready for college, lowering the number who must enroll in remedial courses.

Beyond depressing statistics, the physical and social conditions of many large urban high schools are dreadful. They are overcrowded, understaffed, and often downright dangerous places for students and teachers. Fifty years ago James Conant saw small schools as the enemy of a good high school education because they lacked choices and opportunities for students. Today, these large comprehensive high schools have become the enemy.

The push for small and rigorous high schools specifically targets these big-city schools. Many well-off suburbs have large high schools by small-school standards, yet send most of their students to college. Palo Alto High School in California graduates virtually all of its 1,700 students, and 90 percent go on to college. Even in the big cities, very large, highly selective high schools are also quite successful. Stuyvesant High School in New York City is huge, but unusual because it admits students based on test scores. Out of a student body of 3,200, 99 percent graduate and virtually all go on to college. Clearly, size alone does not determine results.

Where did the high school reform concept originate?

Neither small high schools nor a more rigorous curriculum is new to the world of high school reform. A push for greater academic rigor, especially in math and science, swept the country in the late 1950s and '60s in the wake of the Soviet Union's launch of the satellite, Sputnik, spawning many new math and science textbooks and the Advanced Placement Program. Two decades later, the report *A Nation at Risk* generated a similar wave of attention to academic rigor, inspiring increases in course requirements and tests for graduation.

Small high schools have an equally long history as an out-of-the-mainstream alternative for students—and teachers—including "continuation" schools for students who fail to make it in regular high schools. Often idealistic in their vision, other small alternative schools have persisted, but most do not survive the departure of their founders. In the 1980s, reformers attempted to establish such alternatives on a larger scale. Ted Sizer's Coalition of Essential Schools spawned a number of schools-within-schools in which a subset of teachers and

students, usually self-selected, form a small school within a larger high school. During the same period, New York's Central Park East High School, under the leadership of Debbie Meier, attracted attention by creating a school that could graduate students prepared for college in a district of poor black students, few of whom ordinarily finished high school. Scores of small high schools in New York and other large cities copied the approach of Central Park East.

However, the idea of hundreds of small high schools replacing large ones is recent. The small-schools movement that had already developed strong local roots in big cities like New York, Philadelphia, and Chicago was greatly expanded by the clout of the Bill & Melinda Gates Foundation, which has already invested nearly $1 billion dollars in redesigning high schools.

What problem is high school reform intended to solve?

Creating small, more rigorous high schools is aimed at beefing up the supply of college-ready graduates. This means raising the graduation rate (lowering the dropout rate) and boosting student knowledge so graduates are prepared for college courses. By replacing large urban high schools with small schools and by increasing the courses required for graduation, governors and philanthropists hope ultimately to provide the college-educated workforce that American companies need.

Specifically, creating small high schools is expected to overcome the alienation and poor education pervasive in almost all large urban high schools. With fewer students, teachers can get to know each one. Sixteen-year-old George is much more likely to pay attention to a teacher who recognizes him, and even knows something about his life outside of school than to a teacher who does not even know his name. In a small school community, teachers can work together to create a more demanding curriculum that is more connected to the world and the lives of their students. As a result, students will be motivated to work harder, learn more, and go to college.

Do smaller schools and more rigorous courses work?

Small schools and more academic rigor do not necessarily go together. One can easily imagine a small school with a weak academic program and a large school with a strong one, such as Stuyvesant in New York City.

First, does size matter? In a word, yes; but only in some areas and for some types of small schools. Studies such as the Bank Street College of Education study of Chicago's small schools document some benefits of smallness, including reduced rates of dropouts and course failures and higher grades.[24] In New York City, more than 100 small public high schools graduate on average 90 percent of their students.[25] Small schools are also likely to provide a greater variety of teaching strategies, a safer environment, and more teacher knowledge about individual students than large schools. Increases in test scores have been documented in some studies, but these are not consistent across all types of small schools and tend to show up more in reading than in math. The third-year report of an eight-year evaluation of the Gates Foundation's small-schools initiative finds strengths in terms of a positive learning climate for students and attendance but notes lack of rigor in curriculum and instruction: "[W]e concluded that the quality of student work in all of the schools we studied is alarmingly low."[26]

The benefits of small schools are usually found in those that either operate independently or as a school-within-a-school; that is, those schools chosen by their students and teachers. Moreover, the school-within-a-school approach is effective only when successfully implemented as an autonomous unit.[27] Breaking up a large regular high school into small sub-units, known as "conversion" schools, does not produce the same results.

At the same time, the evidence that large urban high schools do *not* work for the vast majority of students is quite clear. And the common-sense attraction of smaller, more personalized, safer schools is compelling. The challenge lies in creating the schools in ways that yield the desired results.

More discouraging is the evidence on the impact of increasing academic rigor. When graduation requirements in regular high schools are made more stringent, the dropout rate increases.[28] Graduation rates declined during the same period that course-taking requirements increased. Corroboration comes from interviews with students who say math was the final straw.[29] Passed along without ever understanding the subject matter, they just gave up in algebra or geometry. And those who dropped out were more likely to be minority and poor students.

Dropout rates aside, the increases in course requirements for those who stayed in school had no discernable effect on achievement. Researchers are baffled by the fact that sizable increases in the proportion of students taking a college-prep course sequence have not resulted in rising achievement levels on national tests.[30] One likely explanation is the quality of teaching and support for students. Making courses more difficult without ensuring strong teaching would explain this finding. High schools are already hard-pressed to find enough good school leaders and teachers, especially in math and science. And counselors are a disappearing species.

The solution…in our view

Smaller, more personalized environments make a lot of sense, especially because many teenagers' lack of motivation and behavior problems stand in the way of learning, going to college, and getting a job. But the track record of small schools and the challenges to their creation on a large scale argue for pursuing multiple pathways and goals, both for students who drop out and those who graduate.

One solution offered by governors and business leaders—that all students should be required to take Algebra 2—seems unlikely to produce the desired results. Just because many adults with the highest-paying jobs took Algebra 2 does not mean anyone who takes Algebra 2 will end up with such a job. (Just because all dogs have four legs doesn't mean all animals with four legs are dogs.) The key to increased academic rigor is not the number or names of courses, it is ensuring that the courses are relevant and taught well and that students have the needed educational background to learn from them.

Students cannot succeed in algebra, or any other high school course, or in the workforce if they cannot read. According to 2003 scores from the National Assessment of Educational Progress, or NAEP, the reading skills of 38 percent of students about to enter high school (8th graders) are "below basic." This means they might be able to decipher words—read a page aloud—but they cannot understand what they have read. Adding more rigorous courses to the high school curriculum does not speak to this issue. Schools need the resources to provide intensive interventions in reading, starting well before high school.

Rigor has to mean more than "difficult." A rigorous course gets students thinking and working hard—it's not designed simply to weed out those who are not "college material." Such courses require teachers and materials that connect to youths and their world. Linking students to the community, to the workplace through projects, service work, and paid work should all be options. From the Job Corps and the Youth Corp to Talent Development High Schools and the Quantum Opportunities Program, models for such alternatives exist.[31] A student's experience on the job—even selling fast food—can become the basis for tackling math problems and writing assignments. Students should also have options about time. Some may be able to complete high school work in three years, others may need or want five.

"Every kid can graduate ready for college"[32] is an inspiring goal that needs to be bolstered by

Rigor has to mean more than "difficult." A rigorous high school course gets students thinking and working hard— it's not designed simply to weed out those who are not "college material."

alternatives for the hundreds of thousands of students who do not make it. That almost two-thirds of minority students admitted to college fail to get a degree within six years speaks to more than high school preparation.[33] Moreover, the public schools are not responsible for the scarcity of productive jobs for anyone without at least a couple of years of college or the decreasing numbers of slots in many institutions of higher education. The California State University system denied admission to 12,000 students in 2002-03 because of cuts in funding, in spite of an increase in high school graduates that year.[34] In many fields, even college graduates have to deal with the economic reality that companies outsource jobs for a host of reasons that are not related to educational background—cost and motivation being paramount.

As a country that prides itself on providing second chances, more need to be created for the increasing numbers of young people who leave school early or unprepared for a productive future.

Whole-School Reform

A new generation of entrepreneurs and educators is looking to improve learning one school at a time through top-to-bottom overhauling.

Edison schools, Comer schools, Success For All, and KIPP Academies—who would have predicted that brand-name schools would come to be as well-known among urban parents as trademarked sodas and soaps? In cities and largely minority suburbs, these schools—many of which are charters—proudly display their names on buildings proclaiming to the community that they are different from neighborhood elementary schools. Entrepreneurs like Chris Whittle seek profit in Edison schools (more than 157 in 20 states), while academics like Yale University professor James Comer in his School Development Program (more than 700 schools in 18 states) and former teachers Dave Levin and Mike Feinberg in KIPP Academies (38 schools in 15 states) seek no personal or corporate financial gain in their ventures. Thousands of profit and nonprofit schools, however, share two goals: improving the education of poor urban children and reducing the test score gap between white and minority pupils. Rather than change the entire system of schooling in a district, state, or nation, these entrepreneurs seek to revive dreadful schools one at a time. Thus, whole-school reform.[35]

Where did the idea originate?

The optimism of the 1960s that public schools could solve racial and poverty problems had soured by the early 1970s. Urban riots and the war in Vietnam, as well as national research, had raised serious doubts among policy elites as to whether public schools could overcome the effects of poverty and racism. Pessimism led federal officials to reduce funding for urban programs.

Within this gloomy climate for public schools the Effective Schools movement was born. Believing deeply in the value of equity and rejecting the prevailing doubts among policymakers about ever getting better schools, in the early 1980s, a small band of activist researchers led by university researcher Ronald Edmonds identified a handful of big-city elementary schools with poor minority children who had scored higher on standardized achievement tests than would have been predicted by their family backgrounds. These researchers/reformers found a set of common features in these high-performing elementary schools. The set included clearly stated academic goals, concentration on basic skills, order in the school, frequent monitoring of each grade's test scores, and a principal who acted as an instructional leader.[36]

In short, an individual elementary school housing poor minority children didn't have to be unsafe and low-performing; certain features of high-achieving schools could be replicated. Under the right conditions, a hopeless school could be turned around and become a safe, well-organized, and academically high-performing one.

At about the same time, a barrage of national reports linked the poor global performance of America's economy to the poor performance of

U.S. students on international tests. Politicians, corporate leaders, and critics blasted poorly managed, highly bureaucratized public schools for contributing to lower worker productivity, the loss of blue- and white-collar jobs to other nations, and a less competitive economy. As the report *A Nation at Risk* (1983) put it, the United States had educationally disarmed itself in an economic war.

In the shadow of these fears of losing global economic primacy, the Effective Schools model of reproducing common features of high-performing urban elementary schools became a recipe for whole-school reform with the individual school serving as the keystone to national K-12 change.

Throughout the 1980s, suburban districts and entire states installed Effective School programs, all of which identified five, seven, or 10 features of improved academic performance and laid out careful designs for schools to follow. In 1988, the Hawkins-Stafford Elementary and Secondary School Improvement Act directed that federal Title I funds be used for schoolwide improvement for low-income children, rather than pulling individual youngsters out of classrooms and conducting piecemeal, uncoordinated programs within a school. This new schoolwide approach in federal policy and funding accelerated the spread of Effective Schools and other whole-school models.[37]

In 1991, prodded by federal officials and President George H.W. Bush, business leaders created a private nonprofit corporation that underwrote the New American Schools (NAS) project. The corporation was charged with creating comprehensive designs for schools to prepare students for the 21st century. Design competition led to 11 whole-school blueprints to be implemented in more than 500 schools by 1997. These entrepreneurial efforts added to the pool of competing whole-school reforms.[38]

Building on these previous efforts, in 1998 the federal government provided a quarter-billion dollars through the Comprehensive School Reform Demonstration program to districts willing to adopt one or more of 29 different models of whole-school reform. Some urban districts adopted these models. In Memphis, Tenn., for example, with 118,000 students in 163 schools, Superintendent Gerry House required every elementary school to adopt a model that best fit their school. With the spread of parental choice across the nation in the 1990s, public charter schools became a popular way for parents and teachers to launch a Comer school or for Edison Schools Inc. to win a charter from a city or state to take over a school. Whole-school reform—changing one school at a time—became quite a popular reform strategy in urban districts by the end of the 20th century.[39]

What problem is whole-school reform intended to solve?

By the mid-1960s, as a consequence of federal legislation and the civil rights movement, funds flowed into poor, largely minority schools to lift academic achievement. Within a few years, however, it became clear that these dollars had created a jumble of uncoordinated programs, each with its own promoters. Whole-school reform promised an end to the hodgepodge of privately and federally funded programs.

With the growth of the Effective Schools movement and its slow dissolve into whole-school reform a la New American Schools and the federally funded Comprehensive School Reform Demonstration program, the previous clutter of

> **Converting ideas into practice and joining all of the separate pieces necessary to make whole-school reform work takes time, energy, leadership, resources, and, most of all, patience.**

Whole-School Change: Comer Schools

In 1969, Yale University psychiatrist James Comer introduced the School Development Project to improve low-performing schools. One of the few whole-school designs with evidence of effectiveness according to federally funded researchers, the project had worked with more than 1,000 schools by 2005. Today, nearly 300 schools in 18 states are at different stages of implementation.

The theory behind Comer schools, as they are called, is that children's experiences at home and in school deeply affect their social and psychological development, which in turn shapes their academic achievement. Poor academic performance, then, is in large part due to the school failing to bridge the social, psychological, and cultural gaps between home and school. Turning around a school academically depends upon creating a climate in the school where a community of adults and children can work smoothly together to improve academic achievement.

James Comer

Comer schools seek to:

- Develop collaborative working relationships among district administrators, principals, parents, teachers, community leaders, and health care workers.

- Review problems in open discussion without attributing blame.
- Reach decisions by consensus rather than by mandate.

Each Comer school implements the program differently depending on staff personalities and the students' specific needs. The program relies on staff collaboration and parent involvement to promote expectations of high student achievement.

Governance relies on:

- **The School Planning and Management Team.** Led by the principal, this schoolwide group includes teachers, administrators, parents, support staff, and a child development specialist. As a team they identify where academic improvements need to occur, establish policy guidelines, develop plans, respond to problems, and monitor program activities.
- **The Mental Health Team.** The principal leads this committee and includes teachers, administrators, psychologists, social workers, and nurses. Together they review behavioral patterns within the school and figure out how to solve problems, using relevant child-development principles.
- **The Parents Group.** The goal is to involve parents in all levels of school activity, from volunteering in the classroom to school governance.

Researchers and independent evaluators have scrutinized Comer schools repeatedly and determined that, when the design is fully implemented, the programs have moderate to strong effects on student achievement in largely minority and poor elementary schools.

SOURCES:

• Debra Viadero, "Reform Programs Backed by Research Find Fewer Takers," *Education Week*, April 21, 2004; pp. 1, 18.

• Comer School Web site: http://info.med.yale.edu/comer/about_comer.html

• Thomas D. Cook, Robert F. Murphy, and H. David Hunt, "Comer's School Development Program in Chicago: A Theory-Based Evaluation," (2000), *American Educational Research Journal*, 37(2), 535-97 www.northwestern.edu/ipr/publications/comer.pdf

• George W. Noblit, William Malloy, and Carol E. Malloy, *The Kids Got Smarter: Case Studies of Successful Comer Schools*, (Cresskill, NJ: Hampton Press, Inc. 2001).

• Charles Payne, "'I Don't Want Your Nasty Pot of Gold': Urban School Climate and Public Policy," (Northwestern University Institute for Policy Research 1997). www.eric.ed.gov - report #ED412313

• Debra Viadero, "Report Critiques Evidence on School Improvement Models," *Education Week*, Dec. 7, 2005; p. 15.

programs gave way to single designs (e.g., Comer Schools, KIPP, Edison) tailored to particular schools, presumably increasing the chances of actually doing something about low academic achievement.

Does whole-school reform work?

Whole-school reform has a spotty record. Successes as measured by steady improvement in test scores are the exception. Whatever the model, certain conditions are critical to its initial implementation and ultimate success, and these conditions are often lacking in urban schools. In individual urban elementary schools, whole-school reform has worked in those cases where principals and faculties have agreed to put into practice a particular model (e.g., Accelerated Schools, Success for All), received considerable training and ongoing help over a period of several years, and avoided the high turnover of leadership and staff that plagues most struggling urban schools.

In the majority of schools, however, these conditions are not in place, and whole-school reforms may start and sputter or never even get going. One researcher noted the "disconnect between the thinking of school reformers and the stubborn realities of urban schools," pointing to the negative climate, lack of trust, and racial tensions that characterize many bottom-tier urban schools.[40] Even the developers of many of the whole-school models have expressed disappointment at the rates of success among the schools they have worked with.

The situation is even more dismal when districts have mandated a menu of whole-school reforms from which faculties choose. In Memphis, for example, Superintendent House's successor dismantled the whole-school reform program within a few months of House's departure because of low test scores and internal conflict.[41]

Furthermore, findings from studies of New American Schools (NAS) over the past decade might well leave designers of whole-school reforms depressed. After following more than 100 schools implementing whole-school models between 1996 and 1999, RAND Corp. researchers concluded that the theory pushed by NAS (e.g., whole-school designs could improve a school's performance) was unsupported. The evidence RAND gathered showed conclusively that schools adopting comprehensive models needed district support to survive intact. NAS had also stated that if 30 percent of a district's schools adopted whole-school reform the district would become high-performing and not slide back to its low performance. RAND researchers found that to be untrue in Memphis.[42]

Moreover, whole-school reform has yet to show promise for urban high schools. Even though there are instances of whole-school reform models for high schools (e.g., High Schools That Work), and individual high schools that have transformed themselves, the overall record remains dismal. In fact, whole-school reform for high schools has largely given way to another strategy: converting large urban high schools into several small schools—a reform we describe and analyze in another chapter of this book. (See p. 60.)

The solution…in our view

Good ideas for improving schools are seldom in short supply. Converting those ideas into practice and joining all of the separate pieces necessary to make whole-school reform work—qualified teachers, district help, stable principal leadership, ongoing training for teachers, parental involvement, and other factors—takes time, energy, leadership, resources, and most of all, patience. Without sustained attention to these many factors, the best ideas fall flat or dissolve into disappointment.

The lessons from the past three decades of school reform are clear. Reforms must match the desires and capacities of those expected to implement them. Developers of whole-school reform have learned the need for getting teacher buy-in up front, for having an implementation plan that phases in the model over several years,

and for providing substantial training and support to school staff. In fact, reformers whose models are adopted by many schools often find themselves strapped because they too lack the capacity to provide training and support.

If schools do not have the conditions needed to put a reform model into practice, district leaders or model developers must first work to establish those conditions. In the absence of trust among faculty and some sense of common mission, no whole-school reform can flourish. Models differ in their attention to school conditions and to specific academic goals. Both are important, but neither will succeed if the match is not the right one.

Another factor that advocates of whole-school reform seldom mention is that individual schools that are engaged in re-inventing themselves often need help from the district in not only building up the skills and expertise of teachers and principals, but also in buffering school staff from critics as they go through a few years of turmoil before seeing the fruits of their efforts.

Finally, state and federal policymakers develop nervous tics over the slow pace and inefficiencies of changing one school at a time. "For God's sake," they say, "there are thousands of lousy schools across the country: they have to be improved now; we cannot wait." "And why," they add, "can't we do lots of schools at a time?" Helping a principal and staff at one school for a few months and then moving on to another school to repeat much of the work with another staff is inefficient, says a policymaker eager to move low-performing schools into the high-performing column. Yet, for particular schools at particular times when the conditions are ripe—the right principal, the right staff, a "perfect storm" of reform—what few have imagined happening does occur.

All of these factors make whole-school reform a potentially important, but rarely realized solution for low-performing schools.

The Class-Size Conundrum

Reducing class size appeals to parents and teachers,
but the concept comes with high costs and
questions about the truly essential qualities
of a flourishing classroom.

Would you want your 1st grader in a class of 15 students or 30 students? Would you rather teach 20 or 30 students? The notion of fewer students per class carries tremendous gut appeal for parents and teachers alike. Few strategies for improving achievement are embraced as enthusiastically as reducing class size. Students receive more individual attention. Teachers can spend more time teaching instead of managing and disciplining. Struggling students are less likely to fall through the cracks.

However—and it's a big however—reducing class size is among the most expensive reform strategies because it requires more of the most costly resources in education: teachers and classroom space. Do its benefits justify such major expenses? Do students actually learn more in smaller classes?

Where did the idea originate?

In the late 19th century, classes in big cities had from 50 to 75 students. In the early 20th century, education progressives introduced the idea of focusing on the individual child, which drew attention to reducing class sizes. These days, class sizes range from 15 to 40, depending on the locale and grade level.[43]

Today, reducing class sizes appeals intuitively to parents and teachers: the fewer students in a classroom, the more attention each will get; and more attention will lead to more learning. Small classes are easier to manage from the teacher's perspective. From the parent's perspective, the child is less likely to get lost and fall behind.

Support for small classes is strongest in the earliest grades. Results from a well-publicized study of class size in kindergarten through 3rd grade in Tennessee in the 1980s has been taken as proof that students learn more in smaller classes. The study found that students do learn more when class size is under 17. In fact, minority students gained more than majority students in the first two years of the study and maintained that edge for the second two years.[44] And, the advantage persisted years later.[45] Because the Tennessee study is one of the few randomized experiments to take place in education research, its results are viewed by many as conclusive evidence that small class size can increase both achievement and equity.

What problem is reducing class size intended to solve?

Large classes pose myriad problems for teachers, parents, and students. Smaller classes do not guarantee more individual attention, but they are at least a necessary condition for it. From grading student work to organizing classroom activities, more students also usually means more work for the teacher. Organizing students in

Quality of teaching is critical. Students are usually better off in a class with 30 students and really good teaching than in a class with 20 students and poor teaching.

groups, engaging students in projects, providing different activities for different students—all are more difficult with larger class sizes.

Although most class-size-reduction debates and policies focus on the early grades, middle grade and high school teachers must also limit the amount of work they assign. Imagine a typical high school English teacher with five classes of 35 students each. Grading a four-page essay means carefully reading and marking 700 pages of work. Even at a good clip—say 30 seconds per page—this translates into six hours of work. A more reasonable minute-per-page is close to 12 hours. No wonder such assignments are rare.

The more students, the more discipline problems, and the more a teacher's time is spent on classroom management instead of teaching. The more students, the less likely a teacher will notice when a particular student gets stuck, and the less likely a teacher will be able to answer every pupil's questions.

Does reducing class size work?

Yes and no. Smaller classes, especially in the early grades, can make a big difference, but only if they are quite small. Studies of class size, including the Tennessee study, demonstrate higher achievement when classes contain 17 or fewer students for several years in a row. The Tennessee study suggests that the benefits make their biggest

impact in the first two grades and that the effect lasts throughout a child's school years. The effects were the greatest for minority students in the first two years of school. This is the time when students need to learn a variety of new behaviors and social skills to function in a school setting, as well as academic content.[46]

However, states and districts typically can afford only to shrink classes in the first few grades of elementary school a little bit—from 30 to 28 or even as low as 20, as California has recently done. But few if any places can afford to guarantee classes with fewer than 20 students.

When classes have 20 or more students, the evidence of improved learning is not convincing. One reason may be that not enough teachers know how to teach in ways that take advantage of small classes. Another explanation is that the quality of the teaching generally matters more than the number of students. Students are usually better off in a class with 30 students and really good teaching than in a class with 20 students and poor teaching.

Sudden shifts to smaller class sizes also cause unexpected problems. California's statewide class-size-reduction law, passed in 1996, had the effect of increasing the gap between poor and rich districts. Reducing class size to 20 children in kindergarten through 3rd grade in every school in the state meant that every school had to hire new teachers and find additional classroom space—a boon to the portable classroom industry. This dramatic increase in demand for more teachers resulted in districts hiring many teachers without credentials. Most of these uncredentialed teachers ended up in schools serving the most disadvantaged students.[47]

The solution...in our view

Given the huge expense of reducing class size, it is not a realistic option for most school systems. However, several solutions are worth considering. One is to reduce class size only in schools with students who will benefit the most: schools with predominantly poor and minority students. Within these schools, the first priority should be the first two grades. In fact, Tennessee put the findings of class-size research into practice in just this way. The state funded smaller kindergarten through 3rd grade classes in 16 of the state's poorest districts. These districts improved their statewide ranking from the bottom to near the middle.[48]

Another solution would be to organize students in smaller and larger groups depending on the learning activity. Masterful teachers organize classes into groups, some of which require minimal teacher involvement, freeing the teacher to work intensively with a small group. In fact, some student activities can be done in quite large groups, enabling teachers to work with a few struggling students. The risk is that students working without direct teacher involvement will benefit less.

Because studies of class size do not document the differences in instruction between larger and smaller classes, some researchers suggest that simply reducing the number of students is too simplistic. They argue the need for more understanding of precisely what happens in those classes that causes higher achievement. If, for example, the results stem from more time spent between student and teacher, then it is worth considering other ways in which this might be accomplished.[49]

Ultimately, the greater the emphasis on helping teachers teach better—and providing teachers with help in handling disruptive students, the less class size will matter. Students are better off in a large class with good teaching than in a small class with poor teaching. So investing in better teacher preparation and opportunities for current teachers to keep learning should be weighed against the expense of reducing class size.

More Time in School

A push for year-round schools and extended school days on academic grounds dovetails with working parents' needs, but the key is how those extra hours in school are spent.

If students learn while in school, they will learn more if they are in school longer. So goes the logic. Extending students' time in school makes sense to reformers and policymakers. They assume that adding hours to the school day and days to the school year will result in higher test scores. Moreover, to reduce the test score achievement gap between minority and white students, reformers promote an extended school day and summer school to give an extra boost to students who need to catch up.

Although these reforms are expensive, research studies have found that students who spend more time on learning tasks also score higher on tests. Fortifying the case for more time in school are test results from nearly 50 countries that show the amount of instructional time spent on math and science is linked strongly to achievement scores.[50]

Just how much time do American students spend in school? Typically, nearly 50 million students go to public school from five to six hours a day 180 days a year. Generally, schools open and close about the same time each day across the country. From mid-afternoon to dinnertime each day and all day during the summertime, working parents—now the majority of moms and dads— have to scramble to find adult supervision for their children.

When summers and other vacations are added up, children spend 80 percent of their waking hours *out of* school. Surveys find that on a daily basis, they watch TV and play video games as much as they sit in classrooms (nearly six hours). All of that time out of school, much of it unsupervised for large numbers of children, doesn't make sense to most policymakers and many parents. They see other nations that require more time in school than the United States performing better on international tests. As the National Education Commission on Time and Learning concluded in 1994, the "uniform six-hour day and a 180-day year is the unacknowledged design flaw in American education."[51]

So reform proposals for year-round schools, after-school programs, extended school days, fewer recesses for young children, and a longer school year find a welcoming audience among both policymakers and parents.

Where did the idea of increasing time in school originate?

The traditional nine-month school calendar with a summer break comes from the 19th century agrarian origins of tax-supported public schools. Farm families needed extra hands to help out at critical times of the year. As the United States became industrialized and urbanized, challenges to a farm-based school calendar arose prior to and after World War II, but especially in the past quarter-century as major societal changes arose in family composition, many more mothers entered the labor market full time, and American students recorded lackluster performances on international tests. Yet the traditional calendar persists.

Most efforts to increase the amount of instructional time have taken the form of longer days, a longer school year, summer school, or year-round schools, which actually change the structure of the school calendar.

In 1988, 13 percent of all public schools offered extended-day programs such as after-school centers; a decade later, 63 percent did so. Many charter and for-profit schools offer more time in school than regular public schools. Knowledge Is Power Program (KIPP) schools across the country, for example, start school at 7:30 a.m. and close at 5 p.m. on weekdays, are open four hours on Saturday, and a month during the summer. Seventy-four percent of charter schools in Massachusetts, New Jersey, and Illinois are open at least 15 percent more than regular public schools.[52]

The first American year-round school (varied calendar versions exist) opened in 1976. Today, there are just over 3,000 year-round public schools (less than 4 percent of total schools) in 46 states (the most located in California) with two-thirds of these being elementary schools.[53]

Under pressure to increase test scores and close the achievement gap, educators have imposed limits on nonacademic activities during the day to increase the amount of instructional time. As the Atlanta superintendent of schools who got rid of recess in elementary schools in 1998 put it: "We are intent on improving academic performance," he said. "You don't do that by having kids hanging on the monkey bars."[54]

What problem is spending more time in school intended to solve?

More time in school offers solutions to a host of problems that result from the expanding global economy and consequent pressures to increase test scores. The No Child Left Behind Act also puts pressure on schools to increase test scores for all students. Increasing instructional time, by adding time or subtracting nonacademic activities, could be one solution.

Closing the achievement gap ups the ante. The lowest-performing students must increase their rate of learning for the gap to close. Reformers propose more instructional time for the lowest-performing students as a way of boosting their achievement. Some research suggests that poor and minority students forget more over the summer than their counterparts who have more opportunities to learn in their homes, at summer camp, or on vacations. Reformers argue that more learning time for these students in the summer can keep the achievement gap from increasing during these months.

With more parents working to maintain their standard of living, more time in school is also a way of easing intense pressure of finding satisfactory child care.

Does more time in school work?

Researchers have tried to show a link between more time in school and test score improvement. It is tough for researchers to disentangle the payoff in test score gains of increasing the time spent in school (or after school) from other innovations that usually accompany changing school schedules. New texts, new technologies, professional development of teachers, changing school populations, turnover in teachers and principals— all factor into the year-to-year mix of test score gain, stability, or loss. So the benefits have been hard to prove—except for one point.

Evidence from many studies demonstrates that simply adding hours to the day, days to the year, reducing recess, or launching a new after-school program does not in itself yield improved academic achievement. What matters is how that time is spent in the classroom. Adding 60 minutes of instruction a day, five or 10 days to the school calendar, switching to a year-round calendar, or extending the school day does not necessarily

Efforts to improve classroom practice must include increased professional development for teachers in subject matter and teaching skills.

translate to students focusing on academic tasks. What counts is the actual time students spend learning subject matter and skills.

In fact, even a high-quality summer program for low-performing students cannot substitute for effective instruction during the school year. Students who benefited from Chicago's Summer Bridge program returned to their low performance the following school year.[55]

The solution…in our view

If more time in school is more of the same, the goal of increased achievement will not be realized. To convert more time in school into classroom academic gains, the teacher remains the gatekeeper. Longer school days, after-school programs, and summer programs can increase student achievement only if teachers succeed in motivating students to attend and provide high-quality instruction. Thus, efforts aimed at improving classroom practice must include increased professional development for teachers in both subject matter and teaching skills.[56]

To the extent that options for additional time are voluntary, as is true with many after-school and summer programs, those who need it the most may not attend. So another part of the solution is extra efforts to provide the help and support families need to be sure their children attend.

Although strong evidence for increased gains in test scores is missing, extending the day and adding days to the school calendar can be justified on grounds of cost if teachers fully participate in making the additional time academically worthwhile with better-prepared lessons and a more engaging curriculum. Paying teachers for 12 months rather than nine, for example, means that summer school programs are staffed with experienced practitioners. Twelve-month contracts also mean that teachers have more time to prepare classroom materials, upgrade their skills, and work with others to improve instruction.

Although reformers propose more time in school as a way of increasing student achievement, additional time also can be justified on other grounds: the relief it can bring to parents to know that their children are safe in settings where staff care for their well-being and can provide educationally enriching experiences.

Moving from Middle School to K-8

Low test scores and recurring disciplinary problems
are leading some to think that reorganizing
elementary and middle schools
into K-8 schools is the solution.

"Here we are," said former Cleveland Superintendent Barbara Byrd-Bennett, "taking children at 10—at their most delicate—and ripping them from a stable [elementary] school environment. Then we put them in a new [middle] school where they move from class to class, learning to deal with a series of other adults while they were learning to deal with each other." In 2002, Byrd-Bennett sought to move students out of 25 middle schools (grades 6-8) into elementary schools, grades K-8. Why? District data convinced her that when students left the 5th grade and entered middle school, test scores fell while school absences and suspensions rose.[57]

Cleveland's school chief was not alone in seeking more K-8 schools. Since the late 1990s, efforts to create more K-8 schools while closing middle schools have slowly spread across many cities. Often spurred by low scores on international, national, and state standardized achievement tests, as well as longstanding difficulties in dealing with children ages 10-14, reorganizing elementary and middle schools into K-8 schools has become an attractive reform. Of the 30,000 elementary schools in the United States today, about 10 percent are K-8. The current reform will likely swell that number.[58]

Reconfiguring grade levels as a reform strategy is not new. The question is whether its underlying assumption holds up: that a new configuration of grades into K-8 can provide a wholesome education for early adolescents while remedying low academic achievement and misbehavior.

Where did the K-8 schools idea originate?

In the beginning, there was the one-room schoolhouse. In the early to mid-19th Century, anywhere from five to 35 students ages 4 through 18 gathered in the local schoolhouse each day for a few months a year to recite their lessons. In the early 1800s, however, one-room schoolhouses in growing cities like Boston, New York, and Philadelphia became overcrowded and unwieldy. Reformers adopted another form of organization called the age-graded school.

The idea was imported from Prussia and first installed in Quincy, Mass., in the 1830s, where an eight-room building housed children in grades 1-8 (kindergarten reformers didn't succeed in adding space for 5-year-olds in public schools until the early 1900s). Noted for its efficiency in bringing together anywhere from 400 to 600 children in one building (instead of 10 or more one-room schools), the innovative 1-8 school had a teacher assigned to a separate classroom for each grade. In that classroom, she taught a prescribed portion of the curriculum. Like climbing a ladder, students had to master the subject matter and requisite skills satisfactorily before advancing to the next rung or grade. By 1900, the 1-8 school (soon to become K-8) became the standard across the country. By 1920, four of every five high school students had attended a K-8 elementary school.[59]

But there were problems. Many students in the early grades left school at a very young age, particularly in cities where immigrant families sent their children to public school. Juggling a new language and culture, many students stumbled over academic work, attended school infrequently, and repeated the same grade over and over. By age 12, most urban students gladly left school to help support their families, finding jobs plentiful in a rapidly expanding industrial economy. Critics of the K-8 graded school pointed out the wastefulness of tax dollars when 10-year-old students were still in the 1st grade and barely literate 12-year-olds left elementary school for good. To reduce "laggards" and high attrition rates in elementary school while expanding access to more education, early 20th century reformers expanded the role of the school beyond the academic life of its students. They introduced school lunches, after-school recreation, medical and dental exams, and practical subjects; they sought to shift classroom instruction from traditional teacher-centered activities to student-centered ones connected to the real world.

In the early 1900s, these reformers also promoted the newly invented junior high school (grades 7-9). They blamed the rigid traditional teacher-centered K-8 elementary school for driving 12-year-olds to drop out. Advocates of the innovative junior high school saw these new grade organizations as ways of motivating early adolescents to stay in school, advance to high school, and earn a highly prized diploma. Junior highs expanded rapidly across the nation. The K-6 and 7-9 school organizations so familiar to today's parents and grandparents became established pillars in the public school system—except in a few districts such as Chicago that retained K-8 schools. By 1960, 80 percent of students attended K-6 schools before moving into junior highs.[60]

Yet a half-century later, another generation of reformers, worried about unmotivated early adolescents and dropouts, blamed junior high school for becoming too inflexible and too impersonal in dealing with the diversity of interests among early adolescents. Far too much teacher-centered academic instruction and aping of high school rituals (proms, yearbooks, etc.) caused many 8th and 9th graders to leave school, these reformers said. Instead of letting young adolescents explore their strengths, the junior high school had become a virtual boot camp preparing them for high school. In the mid-1960s, reformers pushed for a new flexible and personal form of organization called the middle school (grades 6-8 and 7-8) that would let youngsters connect to teachers while discovering their different talents. By the 1990s, most junior high schools had reorganized into middle schools.[61]

Yet, at this time another generation of school reformers, particularly in cities, saw that these reconstituted (and larger) middle schools contained far too many students who performed poorly on achievement tests, got into trouble, dropped out of school, and, in general, turned off to the idea of furthering their education. In an economy where a high school diploma was a necessity for even entry-level workers, this was unacceptable to those seeking equity for poor and underserved minority groups. To these reformers, like superintendents in Cleveland, Philadelphia,

Critics charged that, instead of letting young adolescents explore their strengths, the junior high school had become a virtual boot camp preparing them for high school.

and other cities, dumping middle schools and returning to the K-8 organization would lift test scores, reduce the number of dropouts, and re-engage turned-off early adolescents.

So within less than a century, the K-8 school had gone from the dominant elementary school organization to an outmoded, less desirable form of a graded school to being rediscovered as a solution to serious defects in schooling urban early adolescents.

What problem is K-8 organization intended to solve?

Just as middle schools were created to address poor academic achievement, high absenteeism, and increased disciplinary incidents among young adolescents, the current push for K-8 schools aims to solve the same problems. "Folks have been aware, in achievement terms," said one Johns Hopkins University researcher, "that what happens in the middle grades is disappointing."[62]

To reformers like big-city school board members and superintendents, a reorganized K-8 school retains the personal closeness of the elementary school while still permitting 10- to 13-year-olds to explore their talents. The idea is that students will benefit from being in a school that has fewer students than most urban middle schools and is located in their neighborhood.

Changing grade configurations within schools also solves problems of overcrowded or underused school buildings. In 2005, Jeri Fierstein, a spokesperson for the Yonkers, N.Y., School District, said her district turned three elementary schools into K-8 schools to boost personalization and test scores, and to relieve overcrowded middle schools.[63]

Does K-8 organization work?

Research does not support the claim that K-8 schools, or any particular grade configuration, solve the above problems. Few studies have shown that K-8 schools in and of themselves cause higher achievement, reduced absenteeism, or fewer disciplinary incidents. In fact, in cities such as Chicago, K-8 schools may house K-6 students in one building and grades 7-8 students in another, or in separate wings, creating in effect two separate schools that have little to do with each other. The same holds for middle schools. Reorganization is one thing; it's another to change the culture of a school and its classroom practices. As one middle school principal put it: "If you're not addressing what happens in the classroom, it really doesn't make a difference what grade configuration you have."[64]

A few studies do show that in high-poverty middle schools where low performance on tests is habitual, conversion to K-8 units may improve academic achievement and behavior. However, these studies also reveal that, in the same district, some poor and large middle schools performed as well as high-poverty K-8 schools. Those middle schools had implemented the Talent Development Middle School Model with interdisciplinary teams of teachers, small learning communities, coaches to help teachers, and extra help for students struggling with reading and math. They outperformed K-8 schools and other middle schools in the district. Again, reorganization by itself is not a solution to the school-based issues facing this age group.[65]

The solution…in our view

Raising low academic achievement and reducing discipline problems among early adolescents takes far more than simply reorganizing elementary and middle school units into K-8 schools. Earlier reformers recognized that this in-between population of youths moving from childhood to adolescence required more than shifting grades around. They needed personal attention, experienced teachers who knew their subjects and could build strong relationships with students, schedules that allowed teachers and students sufficient time to work together, and experiences that permitted them to explore their talents in different subjects through forms of instruction that demanded rigor while actively involving students in their own learning.

Both junior high schools in the first half of the 20th century and middle schools in the second half attempted to achieve these goals, but fell far short. For K-8 schools to have greater success, school boards and superintendents will need to pay sustained and careful attention to the distinctive features of this age group in what happens everyday in their classrooms, lunchrooms, computer labs, and hallways.

This cycle of high hopes dissolving into disappointment need not occur again with K-8 reform if promoters build on parent commitment to have such schools in their neighborhood, invest in experienced teachers committed to working with this age group, provide the necessary resources to help both teachers and students grow, and learn from past efforts with this age group to avoid their errors.

Reforming Teaching and Learning

W e began with the system of schooling, moved to school organization, and now we turn to the classroom. System reform policies and changes in school organization both indirectly influence what happens in classrooms. Curricular and instructional reformers have larger ambitions. They want to leave their imprint directly on classroom practice. In this section, we analyze reforms that seek to shape what and how teachers teach and students learn. Topics that touch on the classroom spark considerable debate, which we find in examining reforms in reading, math, and teaching those learning English for the first time. Professional development, the key to actually changing what happens in classrooms, is included as is the use of technology for classroom instruction.

Learning to Read: Phonics Revisited

The ongoing debate over the best way to teach reading may sidestep the more important issue of focusing on the individual child's needs and helping teachers respond appropriately.

Should children know how to sound out words correctly, or should they understand what they are reading? Obviously, the answer is both, yet the so-called "reading wars" make it sound as if one must choose sides.

"Phonics" refers to the connection between written letters or letter combinations and how they sound. Some argue that until students master these connections—until they can "decode" letters into sounds, they cannot learn to read. First, you learn the rules for sound-letter relationships, then you move to reading for understanding. "Whole language" proponents, on the other hand, argue that reading is about making sense of the words, not simply sounding them out. They emphasize reading for understanding while teaching spelling and pronunciation along the way.

In fact, there are many effective ways to teach how letters and sounds are connected and many ways to teach reading comprehension. Yet many children do not learn to read.

Some children take to reading like a duck to water. Typically raised by well-educated parents, in homes filled with books and conversation, these children will learn to read however it is taught. They start school with large vocabularies and once they grasp the basic idea of correspondence between letters and sounds, they take off.

For those who start school with limited exposure to books and small vocabularies, learning to read is much more difficult. Or

consider newcomers, speaking Spanish, Chinese, or one of dozens of other languages, trying to learn to read in English. It is difficult not only because of their backgrounds, but also because English is particularly complicated as languages go. Unlike Spanish or French, English has many more sounds than letters; and, to make things even tougher, the same sound can be spelled in different ways and different sounds can be spelled the same way. Try describing the rule for pronouncing "ou" or "gh" as in: cough, through, though, tough, bough, dough.

For too many children, even those who can pronounce all the words, the ability to understand what they read lags far behind. By 4th grade, when reading and thinking come together in the school curriculum, reading scores plummet. The problem gets worse as students who can't read well reach middle and high school where they are expected to make sense of textbooks in different subjects.

National data from 2005 suggest that only a third of the nation's 4th and 8th graders can be considered "proficient" in reading. Minority and poor children are much worse off. In addition, more than half of black and Hispanic 4th graders tested at the "below basic" level compared with less than a quarter of white students, according to the 2005 National Assessment of Educational Progress (NAEP).[1]

This is the backdrop to the current debate over how best to teach reading. The controversies are especially heated because the federal government has taken sides, promoting not only a phonics-based approach but, in particular, reading programs that are "scripted"—that literally tell elementary school teachers what to do and say each step along the way.

Where did the idea originate?

By the middle of the 20th century, there were two main schools of thought on teaching reading: phonics and look-say. Look-say focused on recognizing words and what they mean rather than the code that connects letters to sound. Some readers may remember: See Dick and Jane. See Dick and Jane run. See Spot. See Spot run.

Look-say was prevalent in the 1940s, '50s, and '60s, relying on books with very simple words. The '70s and '80s saw a return to phonics in many different forms, with claims it was superior to look-say. Throughout, most teachers actually used parts of both approaches. Most children learned to read well—and many did not. Whatever the popular approach of the day, those who struggled with reading tended to come from the least affluent homes with the least-educated parents.

In the 1980s and 1990s the idea caught on that reading naturally develops if children are exposed to good books and guided to learn the sound-letter connections as they run into them. Called "whole language," its philosophy attracted strong adherents and vicious attackers. Advocates sported T-shirts making fun of the limitations of phonics: "Foniks rilly werks." Critics lambasted whole language for allowing students to make mistakes and to use "invented spelling" in their efforts to teach students to write before they could spell.

The 21st century brought a strong backlash against whole language. Critics used the federally supported National Reading Report (2000) as ammunition to justify both a return to phonics and use of reading programs that specify exactly what teachers should do. Although the report itself was limited in scope and modest in its conclusions, the

The root problem is how to teach children to read, especially those who start school behind their peers. The key question is how to figure out what each child needs to become a proficient reader.

more broadly read summary and the rhetoric surrounding the report made claims about the connection between phonics-only instruction and learning to read that the report itself does not make.[2]

What problem is the emphasis on phonics intended to solve?

Phonics-based instruction has the same goal as every other approach to reading: helping children become literate adults. Whole-language teachers are faulted for insufficient attention to phonics. Phonics teachers are faulted for inattention to how children make sense of the words and sentences they read. Each approach tries to compensate for the weaknesses of the other. But the problem remains: a high percentage of children cannot read, and most are from low-income, minority, and immigrant homes. So the root problem is how to teach children to read, especially those who start school behind their peers.

Reading specialists and researchers argue that the issue is deeper than whether one approach works better than another. In fact, along with teachers, most other experts reject the idea that one size fits all. The key question is how to figure out what *each* child needs to become a proficient reader. Researchers who look beneath test scores in reading find that struggling readers have quite

As one researcher noted, students with no experience hearing ideas discussed can go through school without ever understanding what "understanding" is.

different kinds of problems. So the underlying challenge is to pinpoint the stumbling blocks for each child.

Children who have trouble learning to read typically hit one or more of three main obstacles.[3] The first is understanding letter-sound relationships. The second is extracting meaning from what is read, which gets harder and harder as students advance through school. And the third is being motivated to want to read and understand.

Phonics instruction targets the first stumbling block head on. It begins to focus on the second, comprehension, but is criticized for reliance on simple-minded paragraphs and stories that do not require much thinking. Phonics-centric instruction is not designed in itself to motivate interest in reading for children, but instead intends to provide the skills needed to decode words.

To ensure that teachers provide adequate phonics-based instruction, federal officials and several state governments now push for elementary reading programs that dictate the details of each day's lesson, even providing an exact script for teachers to follow. Intended as a solution for poorly prepared and new teachers, such an approach contradicts the importance of diagnosing each child's particular needs. Such diagnosis, however, relies on teachers having the skills to act on the results.

Students need to grasp the fundamentals of reading by 4th grade so they can read and understand the progressively more difficult materials they encounter in their schoolwork.

Even those who master phonics are not necessarily able to handle the more complicated demands of reading in middle and high school courses. So, along with phonics, students need preparation for "reading to learn." Learning to read and reading to learn are not the same. As one researcher noted, students who have no experience hearing ideas discussed can move through school without ever understanding what "understanding" is.[4] High school students who have not learned to "read to learn" are doomed to failure in most academic courses.

Does 'new phonics' work?

National data on reading achievement for the past 35 years strongly suggest that whichever reading approach is in vogue makes no difference overall. Scores from the National Assessment of Educational Progress show little change since 1971. One exception is a jump in scores for 9-year-olds from 1999 to 2004, too early to reflect changes in federal policy, but perfect timing to reflect the impact of the hugely popular *Harry Potter* books.[5]

This does not mean that there are no better or worse ways to teach reading. Whether the emphasis is on phonics or comprehension, there is no one best way. Both are essential, and either can be done poorly. Students drilled on phonics could sound out many words, but have no idea what they had just said. At the same time, students who needed some basic rules of thumb to translate letters into sounds might never have gotten them in classrooms where poorly trained teachers went overboard on reading for pleasure.

Researchers and educators agree that it is important to focus on explicit phonics instruction in the early grades. But not at the expense of reading, being read to, and discussing words and stories. Like any sport, learning and practicing the individual skills is important. But if years go by without the student ever playing the game, interest quickly disappears. Imagine practicing dribbling and free throws without ever playing a basketball game. On the other hand, throwing a youngster into a game before she has acquired any of the necessary skills could be overwhelming.

Government encouragement of scripted reading programs that emphasize phonics appears to solve one set of problems while causing others. For new teachers, having a set of textbooks and guidelines for what to do and how fast to proceed can be an enormous help. As a top New York City administrator said:

"Instead of everyone trying to figure out their own way in the classroom, which is the way these schools used to work, new teachers in particular need a very clearly defined program that isn't going to change with every new year. ...It's like learning to cook. You learn the basics first, and then you can get fancy."[6]

Yet such lock-step approaches fly in the face of one of the basic tenets of effective teaching: the need to identify where each student gets stuck. A team of nationally renowned reading experts analyzed reading difficulties in young children for the National Academy of Sciences and concluded: "If we have learned anything from this effort, it is that effective teachers are able to craft a special mix of instructional ingredients for every child they work with."[7]

Only a third of high school seniors are considered proficient in reading, according to 2003 national data, and these are the students still in school.[8] Half of black and Hispanic students have dropped out by the time they turn 17, and those who remain—the top half—have the same reading scores as white 13-year-olds.[9] This discouraging picture suggests the need for solutions that go well beyond the federal emphasis on phonics in the early grades.

The solution...in our view

It turns out teaching reading *is* "rocket science." Far from being a simple matter of connecting sounds and letters, reading is about understanding and thinking. Most teachers embrace the view that reading is key to all academic learning and, as a result, they seek to balance the extreme positions.

Educators know that children need the skills to break down a word and that phonics instruction is especially important for struggling readers. They also know that teaching phonics is relatively straightforward. Teaching understanding and thinking is not.

Balance in reading programs is equally important. Leaving it up to teachers to figure that out does not make sense. Nor does telling teachers what to do every minute. Scripted programs may have their place, but most teachers need a better balance between direction on what, when, and how to teach, and the flexibility to respond to the particular needs of individual students. Still, it does not make sense to leave all the work of achieving balance to teachers already pressed for time and, in some cases, without adequate training.

Thus, teachers need better training and better reading programs. They need opportunities to learn better ways to figure out which of many problems a particular student is having and guidance on what to do. They also need experts to turn to for advice when they are not successful. At the same time, students from backgrounds where little reading occurs need preschool and other early-childhood experiences that introduce the concepts of reading and talking about ideas. They also need interesting books to read and the time to read for pleasure as they go through elementary school.

Reforming Math Teaching

Some decry "drill and kill" math while others
dismiss "anything goes" math. Perhaps the answer
lies in drawing from the best of both worlds.

" **I**'m no good at math" "I hate math!"
How many students—and adults—
make this claim? It is almost a badge of
honor in this country. Students can't
wait to be done with required math courses. Even
those who complete all the college-prep courses
often find themselves enrolled in remedial math
when they enter college. For instance, more than a
third of college freshman were not qualified to
take college-level math courses in fall 2004 across
the 23-campus California State University
system.[10]

Education critics complain about the relative
ranking of the United States internationally,
especially on tests that require students to solve
mathematics problems. When the National Council
of Teachers of Mathematics (NCTM) standards were
released in 1989, they spawned the development of
several new standards-based math programs
intended to increase students' understanding of
math. Since 1990, NAEP math scores have been on
the rise, overall and for all groups.[11]

However, gaps in math test scores between
white and minority students and between affluent
and poor students remain large. Algebra I has
become the new "civil right"—the gateway course
to college for minority students—and it is now
often taught in 8th grade rather than the first year
of high school. Among students who do
consistently poorly in math and have grown to
hate it, many shy away from algebra or are
counseled to take arithmetic instead, which is
often called accounting or general math. Sadly,
students who do not go on to college have no other
avenues for learning the kinds of math that could
be useful to them.

Instead of trying to understand why most
students dislike math and fail to learn even the
basics, ardent activists have waged public battles
over how to teach math. On one side are the
approaches favored by traditionalists, politely
referred to as skills-based math, but often derided
as "parrot math" or "drill and kill" math. On the
other side are programs favored by the reformers,
generally called reform or standards-based math—
and frequently dismissed as "fuzzy math" or
"anything-goes" math.

The labels make the two camps seem miles
apart. Yet both sides are actually in considerable
agreement over what students need to know.
Students, they say, need to master basic skills and
procedures, as well as understand underlying
concepts. Without understanding the concepts,
students have no way of knowing *when* to use a
particular skill or formula: for example, when they
have to measure a room to estimate how much
paint to buy or want to make sense of credit card
interest charges.

What sets the warring factions apart is how best
to accomplish these goals. Both sides have
extremists: those who believe learning results
from memorizing facts and formulas, and those
who believe that each child must develop his or
her own understanding and procedures. But most
educators, mathematicians, and the general public
fall in the middle.

Where did the reform math concept originate?

The first wave of mathematics reform began in the early 1950s and accelerated after the launch of Sputnik in 1957. The "new math" was created by university professors who aimed to update traditional mathematics content with newer ideas such as set theory. This reform was short-lived. Some schools actually used "new math" materials, but many used traditional textbooks, which were reissued with new language—for example, replacing "answer" with "solution set"—that lent only the surface appearance of the new math. Few teachers had any knowledge of the new ideas, nor opportunities to learn them, so their teaching remained the same. Those who did change were greeted by parent complaints that they had not learned math this way. In the early 1970s, math teaching went "back to basics" with a vengeance.

After a decade of a back-to-basics focus on computation and procedures, students were no better off. Most were neither very good at problem solving, which they had not been taught, nor very good at the basics which they had been taught.

A Nation at Risk, the influential report released in 1983, prompted the NCTM to issue standards for mathematics curriculum in 1989. The goal was to shift the emphasis from teaching computation and procedures to teaching understanding of concepts and how to solve real-world problems. Learning by doing would replace rote learning. In a typical lesson, traditional math teachers state a rule, give an example, and then assign problems similar to the example. Reform math teachers, in contrast, first provide students with a task and discuss the important mathematical ideas it embodies before giving students problems to solve. For example, to teach adding fractions young students might be asked to figure out how seven people can share six cookies by cutting circles representing cookies into pieces. After several similar examples students would be asked to figure out the general rule for dividing any number of cookies among any number of people. The National Science Foundation

Traditional and Reform Mathematics: Two Approaches to Learning

◼ Traditional mathematics teaching

The teacher tells the class that pi is a constant equal to 3.14 (or 3.1416, etc.) and explains to the class that the formula for the circumference of a circle is pi times the diameter. Students then practice calculating the circumferences of circles with different diameters.

◼ Reform mathematics teaching

The teacher has students measure the diameter and circumference of several circles of different sizes. The students record the data in two columns, and the teacher asks them to look for a pattern across the pairs of numbers. Once they observe that the circumference is always a little more than three times the diameter, the teacher provides the name, pi, its precise value, and the formula.

supported the development of new programs based on ideas like these.

To justify this approach to teaching math, proponents of reform math point out how much both mathematics and the world have changed. More new mathematics has been developed in the past 60 years than the preceding thousands of years. Technology has changed the way math is done, by accountants and engineers, as well as by mathematicians. Together with a greater understanding of how students learn, these historical developments form the rationale for reforming math teaching.

What problem is reform math intended to solve?

Too many students fail to learn mathematics in school, and, for several decades, many students have viewed math as tedious at best. Dropouts point to math as their most discouraging school experience.[12] Almost everyone remembers sitting in a math class where the teacher goes over homework, does a new problem, and assigns a page of problems. A few students "get it," but many do not. Robert Reys, who went on to become a mathematics professor, described his high school experience more than 40 years ago.[13]

"Most of my peers hated math. Algorithms and tedious procedures were demonstrated with little or no explanation of why they work. Sensemaking and understanding were not a part of my experience of learning mathematics. Students left class thinking that math consisted only of dull procedures and rules to memorize."

Similar stories abound today. One student, forced to take remedial math at her community college, said: "My algebra teacher would give us an assignment and tell us to do the homework. The next day she would give answers on the overhead. I never understood how she did it, and she didn't show us."[14]

Today, understanding math is an essential part of being an informed citizen. In the past, adults could manage with minimal math skills. The need to understand math in daily life is far greater than any time in the past. To make sense of poll results, or claims made for new drugs; to file taxes or financial aid applications, or to realize when you are being cheated all require the ability not only to calculate, but also to think mathematically. Calculators can help with calculation—if the right numbers and operations are entered—but they don't help with making sense of underlying ideas.

In this context, reform math aims to increase the number of students who succeed at math. To do so, proponents argue, requires changes in both what is taught and how it is taught. If the content is more closely tied to today's world, and it is taught in ways that foster understanding, then more students will learn more math.

As competition for admission to elite colleges and good jobs has increased, more students are taking algebra in 8th rather than 9th grade. Historically, Algebra I has performed its gatekeeper function well. The majority of poor and minority students were shuttled into business math and consumer math; those who enrolled in Algebra I failed at high rates. With its emphasis on abstract symbols, algebra was intended to weed out those students who weren't "college material." Many of these tracked students continue to be poor and minority. In fact, students from higher-income families are almost twice as likely as lower-income students to take algebra in middle rather than high school.[15] One hoped-for result of reform math is an increase in college-prep math courses taken by minority and low-income students.

Reform math programs introduce concepts like estimating and functions to elementary school students as a way to better prepare them for algebra. In grades 8-12, these programs combine related ideas in algebra, geometry, probability, and statistics to better make sense of the underlying ideas.

Does reform math work?

It is easier to show that traditional math does not work than it is to prove that reform math works. The failure of minority and low-income students to succeed in math and the need for so many students to take remedial math in college demonstrate that traditional approaches are failing. Watching young people try to make change without a cash register that computes the answer is enough to convince most Americans that students are not learning math.

Few studies of reform math programs exist. Those that do show better results on tests of problem-solving, and no worse on computation tests, than traditional math programs. Some evidence points to higher participation of minority students in high school math when the courses link algebra and geometry, emphasize real-world applications, and are taught by teachers who understand math.

Recent studies confirm the obvious: the more math content that teachers know, the better their students do.[16] And the more time teachers spend teaching math, the better their students do. The implications are clear, but have gone unheeded. Most elementary school teachers have little background in math and are likely to give it short shrift. Meanwhile, middle and high school teachers with math backgrounds are in short supply.

While the choice of curriculum can make teaching easier or harder, the bottom line is that the teacher matters more than the program. Good teachers who know math well can work with a traditional math textbook and also use activities that help students discover what concepts like area and perimeter mean. Good teachers can make connections to the real world and across different topics. They can also use a reform math program and augment its activities with practice in computation to build speed.

But what about teachers without the strongest math or teaching skills? Proponents of reform math claim that reform programs make it possible for teachers to learn more math themselves, just from using the materials. However, the authors are presuming that teachers will follow the books closely, and most teachers do not; they pick and choose what makes sense to them. That most

The failure of minority and low-income students to succeed in math and the need for so many students to take remedial math in college demonstrate that traditional approaches are not working.

elementary school teachers end up with a blend of traditional and reform math is not surprising.[17] But it frustrates both traditionalists and reformers who rightly fear that students are missing out on important facts and ideas.

Both traditionalists and reformers are also trapped by the sheer number of topics they must cover. The proliferation of standards and the need for textbook publishers to include them all has led to the most common critique of math courses in the United States: "A mile wide and an inch deep."

The solution…in our view

"I strongly believe that the most crucial step for promoting racial equality in this country is to educate all elementary teachers mathematically," Patricia Clark Kenschaft, a professor of mathematics at Montclair State University, said in 2005, pointing to research suggesting that at least part of the achievement gap between black and white elementary students can be traced to differences in their teachers' mathematical knowledge.[18] She describes working with a group of 3rd grade teachers who did not know the relationship between multiplication and area. In fact, to her astonishment, they did not even know how to calculate the area of a rectangle. After teaching them area and demonstrating that 3 times

5 can be represented as a rectangle with sides of 3 and 5, the teachers wondered why no one had told them this "secret" before.[19]

Without question, most elementary school teachers need to know more math. If students are not exposed at all to ideas like functions and probability in elementary school, they are unlikely to survive high school math courses. Reform math programs are designed to help teachers teach these ideas *if* they have high-quality training available and expert teachers to consult. The programs are challenging to teach well; teachers need strong questioning skills, as well as considerable knowledge of math.

One strategy might be to hire teachers who specialize in math in the early grades so that those teachers who are math-phobic are not forced to teach math. Math knowledge alone, however, is not enough. Teachers at both the elementary and secondary levels also need to entice students to become interested in math, and these teachers should know a variety of ways to explain concepts that are essential for later high school math courses.

Current testing practices contribute to maintaining the status quo in math. The questions on standardized tests and the topics they cover match traditional textbooks and course descriptions. For example, students who learned algebra and geometry together over two years have been known to face an algebra-only test at the end of the first year that included topics they have yet to study. More adaptable test practices are needed.

Finally, states and districts need to invest in developing programs that combine the best of the old and the new—programs that average teachers can teach well and learn from in the process. In addition, math programs need to focus on a manageable number of topics. Providing opportunities to learn something in depth means sacrificing something else. Unless textbooks and tests focus on fewer topics and more on mathematical thinking, teachers will continue to struggle to "cover the material," and students will continue to suffer.

English-Language Learning

The question of how best to teach English to non-English-speaking students is an urgent one because fluency is closely linked to staying in school.

What is the best way for non-English-speaking children to become fluent in English? Should there be classrooms where the teacher speaks only English and all materials are in that language? Or classrooms where students and teacher speak in the students' native language and use materials in that language while adding more and more English as time passes? Or classrooms where students and teachers switch back and forth from English to students' native language during lessons? Policymakers, researchers, parents, and teachers all want answers to these questions.

Other persistent questions need answering also. How long does it take for English-language-learners (ELLs) to speak conversationally? How long does it take ELL students to be proficient in the "academic" English needed to learn math, science, social studies, and literature? Can ELLs maintain the same level of achievement with other students as they become fluent in English?

These are all important questions because, in 2002, nearly 4 million public school children, almost 1 in 12, needed help to become fluent in English. Of that number, three-quarters are Spanish-speaking children, with Chinese and Vietnamese next highest in percentages. And immigration will continue to bring children of all ages who speak languages other than English to public schools.[20]

Bilingual education, in which students are taught in both English and their native language, and English immersion or sheltered English, in which students are taught only in English, provide competing approaches to helping non-English-speaking students learn English. Reformers of different stripes promote each approach, but their arguments are based more on ideology than data.

Yet the questions are urgent because becoming fluent in English is strongly linked to staying in school. Among Hispanics born outside of the United States, 43 percent left school before graduating in 2001, with even higher percentages in urban high schools. Because dropouts are more likely to be unemployed and involved in crime, reducing the dropout rate is crucial to the lifetime success of English-learners.[21]

Where did the bilingual education idea originate?

Initially, U.S. schools offered only one answer to these questions: sink or swim. Elementary school teacher Sam Anaya recalled entering kindergarten years earlier in Oklahoma speaking only Spanish: "I was just thrown in."[22]

For decades, schools placed immigrants into regular English-only classrooms without any language assistance; many districts even banned the use of Spanish in and out of class. Those immigrant children who picked up English swiftly and kept up with their studies survived.

One newcomer recalled arriving in the United States from Germany at the age of 9 knowing only two words: yes and no. After being put into the 4th grade with a few other non-English-speaking students, he recalled that, "after a year of regular schooling we were almost indistinguishable from our native American peers—this despite the fact that most of our parents spoke very little English." Although the German immigrant and Spanish-speaking Anaya eventually "swam"—Anaya became a teacher and taught at the school he once attended—many immigrants "sank" and dropped out of school.[23]

The teaching of English to immigrants has a long history that makes clear that the issue is as much political as educational. In early 19th Century public schools, English was the only language of instruction for native and immigrant children. As more and more non-English-speaking immigrants came to America and sent their children to school, some groups objected. In 1840, German immigrants successfully lobbied the Ohio legislature to pass a law requiring local school boards to offer German in public schools whenever 75 taxpayers demanded it in writing. In Cincinnati, public schools were established where English and German were the languages of instruction in reading, grammar, and spelling in the primary grades, moving on to instruction in English in geography, math, and other subjects. By 1899, there were nearly 15,000 primary grade students splitting their week evenly between a German teacher and English teacher. [24]

Between the mid-19th century and early 20th century, Polish, Italian, Hispanic, and other ethnic groups used their votes to secure either instruction in their language or establish formal study of their languages in school. Thus, bilingualism has deep roots in the public schools.

That ethnic willingness to foster bilingualism politically, however, was challenged repeatedly by native-born Americans after strong surges of immigration (1880-1920) and during economic depressions (1890-1910) that raised fears of competition for jobs. Worries over being swamped by foreign cultures not only led to anti-immigration laws and occasional riots against newcomers, but also to changes in school policies.

Political and business elites believed that the nation was a "melting pot" where immigrants gave up their culture and were forged into Americans as they worked, worshipped, played sports, voted, and went to school. The "melting pot" idea clearly implied English as the only language of instruction. The "sink-or-swim" approach became daily practice in classrooms.[25]

Yet losing one's native language and culture in order to become American caused tensions between immigrant parents and their children. Surely, parents knew that learning English was essential for their children to succeed in the nation that had welcomed them, but many immigrants regretted, even hated, to see children and grandchildren no longer speaking their native tongue or engaging in traditional cultural practices. For decades, that seemed to be the only choice—subtract one's language and culture to gain another. Not until the civil rights movement of the 1960s did an alternative arise that renewed an older but forgotten tradition: bilingualism

Pressures from civil rights groups led Congress to pass the Bilingual Education Act in 1968. The law funded experimental "transitional" bilingual programs that placed children from poor families not fluent in English into special basic skill classes where they would use their native languages to keep up with reading, math, and other subjects while they were taught enough English to transfer to regular classrooms at a later time. A decade later, the U.S. Office of Education was funding 425 projects in 68 different languages. The vast majority, though, (80 percent) were in Spanish. By then, critics charged that bilingual education kept ELL children already fluent in English in special classrooms to maintain native language and culture and keep jobs for bilingual aides and teachers.[26]

By the late 1970s, after a decade of "transitional" bilingual programs, neither policymakers nor researchers could offer clear evidence that this approach was, indeed, the best way to teach English-language-learners. Nor could they determine how long it would take for non-native speakers to acquire both conversational and academic English, and thus assure academic achievement equal to native speakers of English. Even after the U.S. Supreme Court ruled in *Lau v. Nichols* in 1974 that school districts must provide special instruction to children with a home language other than English, the decision did not specify what the instruction should be.

Since the 1960s, state and federal laws have provided alternatives in English as a Second Language (ESL), Sheltered English, and dual immersion programs, in addition to bilingual education.[27] Most recently, to hold states and school districts accountable for helping non-native speakers progress academically and lowering dropout rates, the No Child Left Behind Act requires districts to make "adequate yearly progress"—as measured by test scores—with ELLs. Pressure to prepare English-learners for tests to meet prescribed academic standards has pushed schools to rely on ESL, Sheltered English, and English-only techniques to teach reading and math, rather than bilingual programs. Today, as they have done for well over a century and a half, policymakers, practitioners, parents, and voters continue to debate these alternatives.[28]

What problem is reforming English-language learning intended to solve?

Teachers of English-learner students face a daunting task. They can have a few to an entire classroom of non-English-speaking children of varying abilities and school experiences. Some are literate in their native languages; many are not. They must help these students learn English vocabulary, syntax, grammar, and pronunciation while teaching them to read and do math proficiently.

At the same time, the federal NCLB law

Transitional Bilingual Education, ESL, and Other Approaches

TRANSITIONAL BILINGUAL EDUCATION: Program in which teachers are fluent both in English and students' native language; designated for children who are learning to speak English.

ENGLISH AS A SECOND LANGUAGE (ESL): Programs are conducted mostly in English, but teachers can use native language of students wherever necessary.

SHELTERED ENGLISH: Programs—often part of an English Only approach—are short-term (usually no more than one year) and conducted in English with some help for those learning the language for the first time.

DUAL IMMERSION: Programs where instruction is in English and another language; such programs are open to students fluent in English who want to learn another language and native speakers of the other language.

ENGLISH IMMERSION: Instruction is in English. Classroom lessons are in simple English so that students can learn the language and academic subjects. In some districts, teachers use English 70% of the time and work up to 95-100% in English by the end of the program.

For immigrant children who start school in kindergarten and get help over time with English, progress is evident. But many enter schools later and struggle.

requires that this group of students meet standards each year and make progress toward closing the achievement gap with their non-minority peers. (See Section 1, p. 22.) Yet, how do you both teach a new language and maintain the same, let alone faster, rate of progress as students already fluent in English? As one Arizona elementary ELL immersion teacher said in 2003 on the passage of a state law banning bilingual and ESL programs: "The idea is not to water down the curriculum, but the reality is the curriculum is watered down because students are just trying to learn the language."

For immigrant children who start school in kindergarten and move through the grades with help in learning English, progress in language development is evident. But many students enter their first American school at higher grade levels, even high school, rendering the challenge even greater.

Because bilingual education dates to the civil rights movement and was initially aimed at poor Spanish-speaking families, the issue has become a political one. For example, between the 1970s and 1990s, public concerns over increased immigration from Mexico, Central America, and Southeast Asia grew, particularly when economic recessions threw millions of people out of work. These years saw opposition to bilingual instruction escalate. U.S. English, an organization founded in 1983, lobbied Congress and states for a constitutional amendment to make English the official language of the United States. Although unsuccessful, the

group's efforts, in combination with other organizations, sought alternatives to bilingual approaches to teaching and learning such as ESL, English-only, and variations of both.

In 1998, enough Californians signed petitions to put Proposition 227 on the statewide ballot requiring all instruction in public schools to be in English. Under Proposition 227, children not fluent in English would receive only one year of Sheltered English. A waiver could be granted permitting bilingual instruction if parents wanted it. The referendum passed with 61 percent of the vote. A similar proposition also passed in Arizona (63 percent) in 2000 banning bilingual instruction except for students already fluent in English.[29] Even with this massive backlash against it, bilingual instruction continues under waivers in California and many other states as a way of educating English-learners because some policymakers, researchers, educators, and parents do find the available evidence convincing.

Do bilingual education or English-only programs work?

The current consensus among researchers who have slowly accumulated studies in the United States and Canada is that all the approaches, done well, are effective up to a point. For elementary school children in reading, math, and other subjects, programs carried out with experienced teachers who carefully and systematically teach the material will result in ELLs becoming conversant in English within at least two years.

However, conversational English is not the same as the academic English needed for each subject area. For Spanish-speaking students to match native-speakers in academic areas it takes between five and eight years of work in ESL and bilingual classrooms rather than English-only ones.

When programs provide insufficient help or end too soon, which is all too common, collateral damage occurs. When teachers are poorly trained, or when ESL and bilingual programs terminate language help in one to three years, most English-learners fall steadily behind academically.[30]

Similarly, sheltered English and English-only programs often provide insufficient help and last only one or two years. Not surprisingly, both the achievement gap and the high dropout rate among Hispanic students, according to researchers, are linked to the amount and quality of language instruction children receive early in their school careers.

Because bilingual education and English only have become politicized, there will likely be multiple approaches to instructing English-language-learners for the immediate future. Research evidence will take a back seat. Overheated public debates will need to chill before research and experienced educators' judgments can be brought to bear on the worth of bilingual education.

The solution…in our view

In the hands of knowledgeable and skilled teachers for extended periods of time, bilingual education is demonstrably effective in teaching reading, math, and other subjects to English-learners. However, there are too few skilled teachers, and the problem is unlikely to be solved in the near future.

Similarly, teachers in English-only and sheltered English programs need far more training in communicating efficiently with their English-learners if the students are to have a chance to move beyond conversational English to the mastery they need to succeed in their academic subjects.

The distinction between conversational and academic language is often overlooked or misunderstood by educators and the public. Educators and parents need help in realizing that conversational English is not enough to succeed academically.

Teachers in schools with high proportions of non-English speakers need to learn how to help students with their language development. Parents and their children need opportunities beyond the school day to learn English.

Yet even if bilingual education and English-only programs lost the taint of their political past, it would take more than qualified teachers and solid instruction over time. The majority of Hispanic and many other immigrant children carry the added weight of poverty and family illiteracy. Their challenge is not simply one of learning a new language. To help ELLs grow intellectually, socially, psychologically, and emotionally, public schools have to do much more than provide effective bilingual and sheltered English teachers.

To make children both fluent in English and academically strong enough to continue and complete school, the job of the schools must expand to include preschool, an extended school day, summer programs, and efforts to involve parents in educating their children. Moreover, there is a need for efforts to remove the stigma of poverty attached to bilingual education and instead use the strengths that children bring to school. For example, such efforts could include using non-native-speaking children as nimble translators for immigrant families and establishing dual immersion programs in middle- and upper-middle-class neighborhoods in schools, libraries, and community centers. Like most reforms aimed at those in low-income families, schools cannot do their job alone. [31]

Redesigning Professional Development

To be successful, high-quality professional development will require investment in training those who teach the teachers.

Asked about her experience in a weeklong summer institute performing experiments in physics, a middle school teacher announced: "This is much better than professional development."[32] Almost a dirty word among teachers and parents alike, professional development, teacher in-service, staff development, training—whatever the label—has come to mean wasted hours spent in "spray and pray" or "sit 'n git" workshops. Teachers traipse across town to listen to an inspirational speech or presentation on the latest hot topic. Worse yet, school is out for a half-day or a full day sending parents scrambling for child care.

The idea that professional development is supposed to be valuable continuing education for teachers somehow fell by the wayside. Yet today it may be more important than ever. Schools are under the gun to raise student achievement, which can happen only if teachers learn to improve what they do. As U.S. Secretary of Education Margaret Spellings put it: "If all you ever do is all you've ever done, then all you'll ever get is all you've ever got!"[33]

So the question is, how do teachers get better? Testing and accountability put pressure on educators to improve, but this pressure has to translate into strategies for helping students learn more. Analyzing test scores is one thing; knowing what to do to increase them is another. In theory, high-quality professional development should help by arming teachers with more knowledge about the subjects they teach and how students learn.

The reform view of professional development is the opposite of the one-shot workshop. Professional development is now expected to combine intensive summer institutes that bring teachers up to date on content and understanding with a variety of on-the-job opportunities for learning and help. It is based on the idea that teachers, like other professionals, learn from each other, as well as from experts. Instead of always leaving the school for workshops or courses, reformed professional development aims to create teacher learning communities in schools, bolstered by chances to observe master teachers and get help in the classroom from expert coaches.

Where did the professional development idea originate?

Professional development for teachers in the 19th century was not radically different from much of what is provided today. Superintendents or outside experts offered classes, gave presentations, and ran summer institutes, both to help teachers pass required tests and to improve their skills. These were held in a central location and resembled many of today's one-shot workshops. The people running the system were the ones who decided what teachers needed.

By the 1950s, colleges and universities, as well as school district offices, became the major providers of professional development, continuing the practice of deciding the content "from above." Districts typically required the participation of all teachers in some activities—usually presentations about new policies and requirements; other alternatives, such as university courses, were left up to individual teachers who chose from a menu of "offerings."

Over the past two decades new ideas about how to make professional development worthwhile have multiplied. The impetus for professional development reform comes from several sources. One has been the need to justify investments in continuing education for teachers. When parents run into teachers in the grocery store on "staff development day" or hear from teachers how boring it is, word of mouth seeps up to legislators looking to make budget cuts. Little documentation of the effect of professional development on teachers and students, combined with a few horror stories, makes it an easy target.

Another impetus is the fact that there is a lot more knowledge about teaching and learning today than when many teachers received their college degrees. Teachers are also being asked to teach new topics. In the past, 5th grade teachers were not expected to introduce concepts in algebra and probability. Today they are.

Current ideas about professional development also borrow from the world of business, where on-the-job training is an integral feature of companies looking to improve their workforce. If a company adopts a new method or procedure, all the affected employees are sent off for training to retool, often for weeks at a time. Education has not made these kinds of investments in the past.

Recently, the federal No Child Left Behind Act has thrown its weight behind professional development. Not only are teachers under pressure to improve test scores, but the law also requires districts to spend at least 5 percent of their Title I budgets on "high quality" professional development. Districts in turn must require each school needing improvement to spend 10 percent of its Title I budget on professional development. In fact, the law provides a list of the kinds of activities that would be considered high quality. Included are several buzzwords that contrast with

Publicity of studies of teaching in Japan and other countries advanced the idea of professional learning communities in which groups of teachers in a school meet regularly to create better lessons.

the one-shot workshop approach: "sustained, intensive, and classroom focused."

Specific recommendations for improving professional development have been influenced by studies of "best practices" in successful schools, districts, and countries. For example, one district in New York City raised achievement scores and accelerated the achievement of the lowest-performing students by creating a rich and varied districtwide system of professional development. Each school had literacy coaches who worked with teachers and regular classroom "walkthroughs" as a basis for identifying teachers' weaknesses and matching them with appropriate help and training.[34] The publicity surrounding this success story spawned national interest in coaching for teachers and classroom walkthroughs by principals.

Similarly, wide publicity of studies of teaching in other countries, most notably Japan, popularized the idea of professional learning communities in which groups of teachers in a school meet together regularly to create better lessons.[35]

The convergence of pressure to create more effective professional development with studies that have identified its critical elements has resulted in a long list of "essentials." The list conjures up an image of a teacher enrolled in redesigned university courses, attending one-week or longer summer institutes, observing master teaching for extended

The reform view of professional development focuses content on what teachers know and do and locates activities in the school where teachers can work together.

periods of time, meeting regularly with colleagues to analyze data and discuss lessons and how to improve them, holding frequent discussions with a school coach or mentor, and receiving feedback from the principal and colleagues. In practice, most professional development falls far short of this imagined scenario.

What problem is redesigned professional development intended to solve?

In the big picture, the goal of better teacher professional development is to improve teaching and therefore increase student achievement. Policymakers and reformers look now to professional development as the way to arm teachers with the know-how they need to help all their students learn more. What this amounts to in practice is: creating worthwhile learning opportunities for teachers, overcoming the view of professional development as a waste of time, and figuring out how to provide the kind of time and help teachers need to learn and put new ideas into practice.

Under increasing pressure to raise student achievement, teachers have few opportunities to learn how to get better at their jobs. Most teachers spend their workday in a classroom with students. They have little chance to meet with other teachers beyond official faculty meetings. Reform ideas for professional development are intended to overcome the current weaknesses of teacher

training, classroom isolation, and traditional professional development.

One such weakness is the separation of much teacher preparation and professional development from the classroom. Reformers argue that teachers need ongoing opportunities to improve what they do, and that this can only happen if teachers work together as "professional communities." The idea is that teachers who teach the same grade or subject meet regularly to look at data from their students and discuss how better to teach a particular topic or concept. Such communities are intended to bring teachers out from behind closed classroom doors, making their work more visible to each other.

Another weakness is the one-shot approach—the spray and pray strategy. New approaches are expected to be more sustained and intensive courses or weeklong institutes. Yet another weakness is the lack of just-in-time help for teachers, meaning efforts to observe and give feedback as teachers try something new in the classroom. So reform approaches necessitate having coaches or mentors at the school.

A further weakness of traditional professional development is its generic nature—workshops about how to group students or a new discipline policy or how to write good lesson plans. Reformers urge a focus on the subject-matter concepts teachers teach coupled with how students learn them. Formerly, districts offered professional development as a menu of choices from which teachers could choose to fit their desires or schedules. Now, reformers urge attention to school goals and priorities set by the school or district.

Together, the reform view of professional development focuses the content on what teachers know and do and locates the activities in the school where teachers can work together and get help to improve their teaching.

Does redesigned professional development work?

Whether professional development "works" can be considered in different ways. Is it possible to

Teachers Learning Together

At Paterson School 2, a low-income K-8 school in New Jersey's urban Paterson district, teachers meet weekly in small groups, thanks to clever scheduling by the principal. But the gatherings are far from typical team meetings. Paterson teachers are using an idea borrowed from Japan: lesson study. Every 12 weeks, they tackle a unit in mathematics. The teachers study the concept behind the unit, how textbooks present it, and how the topic is taught in surrounding grades.

Teachers develop lessons and try them out, sharing what works and what does not. They observe each other and record their thinking and what they learned, keeping their notes with videotaped lessons for future reference.

"It's the greatest thing I've ever done personally as professional development," said William C. Jackson, the school's full-time math facilitator.

According to researchers Catherine C. Lewis and Ineko Tsuchida, the lessons studied—research lessons—have five unusual features:

- They are carefully planned by a group of teachers.
- They are focused on a particular learning goal.
- They are observed by other teachers.
- They are recorded.
- They are discussed.

Teachers open their classrooms for analysis—a gutsy move for professionals who have spent their careers behind closed doors. Afterward, they discuss how the lesson went. They might debate whether 5th graders are old enough to understand measurement error or simply tell a new teacher that she needs to talk more slowly. Teachers not only learn, but immediately put their new knowledge into practice.

SOURCES:

• Catherine C. Lewis and Ineko Tsuchida, "A Lesson Is Like a Swiftly Flowing River: How Research Lessons Improve Japanese Education," *American Educator*, Winter 1998, pp. 12-17, 50-52.

• Debra Viadero, "In 'Lesson Study' Sessions, Teachers Polish Their Craft," *Education Week*, Feb. 11, 2004; p. 8.

create the kinds of professional development envisioned by reformers? If so, does it change what teachers know and do? Does it increase what students learn? And, if the answer is yes, is that learning measured on an annual standardized test?

Given this chain of logic, it is hardly surprising that little evidence exists that even high-quality professional development alters what teachers do or raises test scores. If a teacher goes to a two-hour workshop on teaching statistics to 5th graders, no one would expect her to immediately change how she teaches or for her students' test scores to jump immediately as a result.

On the other hand, suppose a district invests substantial money over several years in classes that help teachers better understand probability and statistics and how students learn these concepts. Then it makes sense to ask if, overall, teachers have changed their usual teaching practices and if scores have increased on a test designed to measure the concepts teachers were taught.

Only a few studies have tried to link professional development to altered teaching practices and student learning. Teachers' language skills and knowledge of the subject seem to make the biggest difference in how much students learn.[36] It makes sense that more students would learn more with teachers who can explain well and who understand the concepts enough to answer students' questions and respond with many different examples. Other research finds that the types of professional development that influenced student learning the most were those that taught teachers more about the subject itself and about how students learn the concepts that were taught. This mattered more than whether it happened at the school, included classroom visits, or whether teachers worked together.[37]

But these studies are few, they mostly looked at math and science, and the links to student outcomes are weak. The impact of professional development on test scores is more likely to show up if a test measures exactly what teachers were expected to learn rather than broad assessments of student achievement.

Some evidence suggests that teachers can learn from each other. Schools where teachers work together in "professional learning communities" can see changes in the classroom and even in student learning.[38] But such communities are hard to build and sustain. Among other things, they require free time for teachers to meet and a stable faculty, conditions that are rare, especially in urban districts. And, they need strong leaders to keep teachers focused on important questions; otherwise, the more immediate demands of the job become the topic of conversation.[39]

Researchers also point to the challenges in mounting good programs for teachers. Whether they're discussing statistics or culture or writing, those who teach teachers need to know the concepts well, know how students learn them, and know how to teach adults. This is a tall order. It is not one likely to be met by most providers of professional development, many of whom are textbook publishing companies.

Even with high-quality providers of professional development, teachers are not necessarily attracted to such opportunities. Not surprisingly, many bristle at the implication that their own knowledge is lacking. Moreover, under ever-increasing pressure to raise test scores, they seek quick fixes, not deeper understanding of what they teach.

The solution…in our view

The oft-quoted report *A Nation at Risk* recommended that: "School boards should adopt an 11-month contract for teachers. This would ensure time for curriculum and professional development, programs for students with special needs, and a more adequate level of teacher compensation." Of course, this would require a substantial increase in education budgets.

On the other hand, without major changes in the time teachers have for anything other than teaching itself, it is hard to imagine when teachers would take courses and work together to figure out why some students are not learning. In Japan, for example, teachers spend only 60 percent of their time with students and, by law, cannot teach more than four hours per day.[40]

It takes more than just setting aside time for professional development to be worthwhile. Without good teachers of teachers and well-trained mentors, for example, professional development will not provide much bang for the buck. Without strong teacher leadership and principal support, teacher professional communities will not flourish. Teachers, too, need incentives to reach beyond their current level of expertise. Current priorities are to raise test scores quickly, which works against the ideas embodied in professional development reform.

What is clear is that improvements in student learning must come from teacher learning. Without high-quality professional development, neither is likely to occur.

High-Tech Classrooms

Computers and the Internet hold vast potential for student learning, but it takes careful planning and teacher training for that potential to be realized.

Mrs. Johnson's 5th graders have their eyes glued to the front of the room as she stands in front of the class with her pointer aimed at the center of an erupting volcano. What used to be a blackboard is now a whiteboard able to display the Web site she has accessed on her computer. The classroom discussion about the density, color, and speed of lava flows is no longer a purely theoretical one. Students are about to turn to their laptops to begin their reports with access to several Web sites on volcanoes. Sifting through information and organizing their thoughts is still difficult, but the work of gathering information and producing written text is vastly richer and more efficient than it used to be.

This scenario suggests the appeal of technology. The combination of today's small, powerful laptop computers and the vast resources of the Internet was unimaginable even 10 years ago. Individual examples of powerful uses of computers abound as do hopes that technology can do what mere humans cannot: increase the efficiency and effectiveness of teaching and learning, and, at the same time, prepare students to use the tools they will find in the workplace.

Yet computers have not really "caught on." In spite of the increasing numbers of computers in school and almost universal access to the Internet, regular instructional uses are the exception. And even where they are used, student performance has not skyrocketed. Why is this, and what's the prognosis for the short run and the long run?

Where did the idea originate?

Expecting technology to solve a host of education problems has a long and dismal history. From film projectors early in the 20th Century to television and then computers, reformers dreamed that these new technologies would revolutionize teaching and learning. Not only would students be more motivated by the entertainment value of the new media, they would learn more with greater efficiency.

The anticipated revolution from use of technology did not pan out. Film projectors languished in closets; televisions and videocassette recorders sat in classroom corners, occasionally used.

The advent of personal computers and powerful software in the 1980s offered a whole new array of possible educational uses, from word processing to arithmetic drill and practice. However, it was the arrival of portability and Internet access in the past decade that has transformed the vision of technology from that of performing traditional tasks more efficiently to making fundamental shifts in what is learned and how it is learned. Now students can travel on a virtual spaceship to see different views of the planets; they can even control a camera on the Space Shuttle by tracking the shuttle's orbital path and selecting points on Earth to photograph, which are then posted on the Web.

Policymakers, business leaders, and educators share some version of this vision. The federal

Although the presence of computers in schools has increased dramatically, uses are neither as widespread nor as revolutionary as expected.

government, states, and districts have invested billions of dollars in wiring schools to provide Internet access. Policymakers and business leaders tout the virtues of the new technology and entice schools with donations of hardware and software and occasional training on how to use them.

What problem is technology intended to solve?

Reformers believe computers can enhance teaching and learning and access to information for teachers and students. From software with simulations of science experiments to drill-and-practice games, computers can in theory provide new opportunities for learning as well as motivate students to want to learn.

Reformers also believe that computers can help teachers become more productive through electronic versions of grade books, report cards, attendance, and other time-consuming record-keeping tasks. The time saved can be spent on activities directly related to teaching. Moreover, access to the Internet could provide teachers with more ideas and resources for preparing exciting lessons.

The same kinds of productivity tools used in the business world can also help students be more efficient. Word processing enables more editing of writing, as well as neater reports with correct spelling. Graphing calculators replace the tedium of plotting points on paper, helping students focus on the big concepts instead of the mechanics.

Whatever their application, students who use computers become familiar with tools common in the workplace, which could be particularly advantageous for students who might not have access to computers at home.

Does access to computers work?

Not yet. Schools have deployed computers in labs, media centers, and classrooms. Nationally the presence of computers jumped from one computer for every 125 students in the mid-1980s to one computer for every five students in 2002.[41] The percent of classrooms with Internet access grew from 3 percent in 1994 to 93 percent in 2003.[42] Although the presence of computers in schools has increased dramatically, uses are neither as widespread nor as revolutionary as expected.

After spending $30 million on computer technology, somewhere between two-thirds and three-quarters of the teachers in Louisville, Ky., do not regularly use computers in their lessons, according to the district director of technology.[43] Similarly, a report on uses of technology in Chicago's public schools noted that such use is "at a rudimentary level" and that "most schools have not substantially integrated technology into students' coursework," in spite of the fact that most students and teachers believe that using computers and the Internet brings academic and occupational advantages.[44]

The hope that the potential of the Internet and portability would radically change how teachers teach is still only a hope. In fact, where technology is used, it tends to be used to support the kind of teaching already in place. Several studies have shown that teachers of middle-class students are far more likely to use technology to enhance thinking through simulations and applications in contrast to drill and practice for low-income and minority students.[45]

Although some teachers' tasks are more efficient with computers, these efficiencies do not necessarily translate into more attention to students. And, overall there is scant evidence that computer use per se results in higher test scores.

Today's students know how to download music files, send email and instant messages, and use search engines, but they don't know how to read and think critically. According to Lorie Roth, a California State University administrator: "Every single [student] that comes through the door thinks that if you just go to Google and get some hits—you've got material for your research paper right there."[46]

Wireless hand-held and laptop computers already exist in schools replacing older technologies. Newer devices will continue to appear and spread throughout schools, if they can afford them. But no evidence suggests that these information and communication tools will magically create better teaching and learning.

The solution…in our view

Improving classroom teaching and learning requires far more than a technical solution. In those unusual places where technology truly enhances teaching and learning, districts have developed strategic plans for using technology in classroom instruction and invested significant dollars in teacher professional development.

Information and communication tools can surely help teachers and students do the hard work of teaching and learning, but they cannot replace the all-important connection between teacher, student, and content. The vast resources of the Internet and thousands of software products are no good to teachers without time and help in figuring out what fits a particular lesson for a particular group of students. If teachers have few opportunities to learn how to use the technology in ways likely to benefit students, the technology will be more hassle than help. Knowing that electronic devices cannot in themselves transform teaching and learning in schools, then, is an important first step in returning the central focus to teachers and students rather than technology.

With investments in teaching teachers, the potential for technology to add value grows, provided the technology is easy to use, in the classroom, and in working order. Technology can enhance teaching and learning, but only if the teacher sees the connection to the lesson, knows what to do with it, and decides it is better for students than the existing lesson.

What Can Reformers and Taxpayers Do?

Reformers care about making public schools better, especially for students at risk of failure. Whether they work in the federal government, state capitals, foundations, universities, corporations, teachers' unions, school boards, or local government, all believe better schools are critical to offering students more promising futures. The problems reformers tackle are real, complex, and tough to solve. The ideas they promote are often good ones and their intentions worthy. Yet reform policies too often go awry as they wend their way into schools and classrooms. The gap between policy and practice remains vast.

So, what can be done to help policymakers and informed citizens turn good school reform ideas into sound policies with a real shot at success? Based upon our analysis of 20 different reforms, we have distilled a set of guidelines that we believe will assist citizens and educators, as well as policymakers from Congress to school boards. Some of the rules apply more to those who produce reform ideas and policies (policymakers and advocates); others are more relevant to those who consume them (educators and parents).

Our advice is organized under the three key questions we raised in the Introduction: Does a reform make sense? Can the reform actually work in classrooms? Are the conditions for success in place?

Does the reform make sense?

This means looking beyond the hype to the underlying logic and assumptions that connect a reform to the promised results, usually increases in achievement test scores. How does one go about this?

Don't swallow the hype. All claims about reforms over-promise. Elected and appointed policymakers alike exploit criticisms of public education. To gin up support for reforms, they overstate problems: the schools are failing, we rank far behind other countries, teachers are unqualified. And they exaggerate claims: no child will be left behind, competition through choice is the answer, all students will reach high standards. Reforms are cloaked in the language of "research based," "evidence based," and "best practices," whether or not a shred of evidence exists in support of an idea. In an era of high-stakes testing, proposed reforms guarantee increased test scores with or without any track record of success.

Programs peddled as miracle cures nearly always fail to deliver desired results and therefore disappoint. Disappointment breeds cynicism and helplessness. Policymakers and advocates need to shrink their over-promising on what reforms can deliver and lower the volume of attacks on what is wrong with our public schools. At the same time, educators and citizens need to be skeptical of the hype and press for more truth in advertising about what it takes for a proposed reform to succeed.

Kick the tires. Do the logic and assumptions of the reform hold up? Reforms aim to increase student achievement, yet most are targeted many steps removed from the classroom. Reconfiguring grade levels, ending social promotion, and merit pay, for example, are all promoted as ways to improve teaching and learning, but the path from each to better teaching and higher test scores is far from clear.

For example, the federal No Child Left Behind Act allows for states to remove the superintendent and school board, that is, to "take over" a district

Implied Chain of Logic of School Reforms

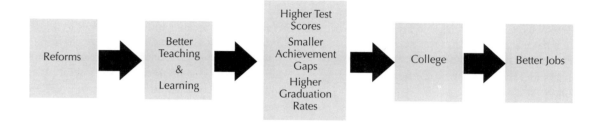

in which many schools have failed repeatedly to improve academically. The unstated assumption is that there is a cadre of highly trained people who can step in, shape up the central office administration, and somehow transform schools in ways that raise test scores and increase high school graduation rates. However, these people do not exist. If they did, one would hope the state would have dispatched them before years and years of district failure.

Policymakers assume cause-and-effect links between reforms and promised results that rarely exist. Most current reform policies rest on the same chain of logic: educators will put policies into practice, which will lead to better curriculum and better teaching, test scores will rise and the gap will narrow, more students will go to college and, as a result, get better jobs. Standards, accountability, charter schools, small high schools—all are expected to improve teaching and learning so scores will rise and students' futures will be rosier. But, in reality, the links between these pieces are not very strong.

The above illustration represents this presumed chain of logic. At the front end, the first arrow on the left suggests that a reform will change what happens in classrooms. The belief that any reform, say, high-stakes testing or small high schools, will lead to better teaching in the absence of a host of other supporting conditions represents the first weak link. This assumption falls into the "and

then a miracle happens" school of policymaking.[1]

Teachers can do more or less of what they already do, but they cannot start doing something they do not know. If 6th grade teachers don't have any way of learning what probability is and how to teach probability, for example, and if they do not have adequate resources such as a strong curriculum and materials for their students, their teaching is unlikely to change even if test scores are low and penalties are lurking around the corner.

Similarly, the links in the middle of the chain of logic above are tenuous. The connection between better teaching and learning and higher test scores, smaller achievement gaps, and higher graduation rates is weak without other elements, including tests that measure more of what matters and efforts to help students stay in school. The link from these outcomes to college is also weak, assuming much about students' preparation, access to, and resources for college.

Federal, state, and district policymakers and reform advocates can—and should—provide solid arguments and evidence linking their proposals to promised outcomes. The public must press policymakers to state clearly the assumptions and steps from the reform to the expected result.

Avoid funnel vision. The chain of logic represented above narrows the picture for the future of students. Fixating on test scores as the only accepted measure of learning is the first narrowing of the funnel, much like looking through a keyhole and seeing only part of what's going on in a room. At the end of the chain the funnel narrows even more, pointing to only one of several desirable outcomes of schooling: better-paying jobs. Other historic goals that the public schools have served for decades such as civic engagement, building community, and molding character disappear in the single focus on economic productivity.

This singular focus on academic standards as measured solely by standardized test scores and high-paying jobs seems to have become an article of unquestioned faith held by rich and poor, minority and white, parents and citizens, policymakers and practitioners. Not only is the focus on economic productivity a narrow one, it ignores labor market realities. Consider that unemployed older adults are taking jobs that high school graduates used to take and college graduates are facing competition from lower-paid college graduates working remotely in India and other distant locations. And having academic skills is not the end-all of schooling. Employers want graduates who are punctual, reliable, can talk easily with customers, and who are motivated enough to teach themselves by reading a manual.[2] Moreover, the sole focus on college graduation as a steppingstone to better-paying jobs ignores the many students whose chances of staying on that path are small.

Policymakers can support investment in better tests that look at a broader range of what students can do and avoid policies that rely on single measures. Taxpayers, too, can insist on more than one test and can raise questions about what job opportunities really exist and how students can learn the values and social skills that employers seek.

Can the reform actually work in classrooms?

Readers should wonder whether reforms require teachers and students to change in ways that are possible. For instance, does the reform connect to what happens in classrooms? Is the reform built on

what we know about implementing new programs? Does the reform presume that "one size fits all" and that all teachers will put in place new programs, no matter what they are?

Where's the beef? For reforms to result in higher student achievement, changes must occur in classrooms. What happens between teachers and students *is* the "beef" of school reform. Simply mandating a new curriculum, however, does not automatically result in teachers changing what they do. And for good reason. Researchers have found that teachers are already making hundreds of decisions a day, motivating and responding to individual students, answering questions, grading papers, and performing dozens of other tasks related to their classes. In addition, teachers know that parents and principals expect them to maintain order, teach the required content and skills, model moral character, and transmit the community's core values. Moreover, these expectations apply to students who are not there by choice, making teachers' jobs that much more demanding.

Any reform aimed at improving student learning depends wholly on how much teachers understand the reform, believe that it will help students learn more and better, and can tailor the reform to their classrooms. If the teacher's perspective is ignored, reforms are less likely to be embraced where it matters the most. Involving experienced educators in designing and choosing reforms increases the likelihood that the reforms will be put into action. Policymakers can invite representative educators to play this role, and taxpayers should insist that they do so.

It's the implementation, stupid. Policymakers neither run schools nor teach students; they make policy for both from afar. Whether the policy is a new program or a new way of operating, the ideas are only as good as those who put them into practice. In fact, it turns out that how well a program is implemented can matter more than what the program is. A famous evaluation, called the "Follow Through Planned Variation" experiment, tested a number of different early elementary programs by getting several schools across the country to try each one. One of the key findings, too often ignored today, was that the differences in results from one school to the next *using the same program* were bigger than differences in results between the programs being compared.[3]

Certainly, some programs are better or worse than others. Assuming that a concept has some merit, however, its specifics are often less important than what individual teachers do with it. At one extreme, teachers can ignore a program, which they may do if it does not make sense to them. At the other extreme, teachers can be excited enough by a program to put extra energy and resources into tailoring it to fit their students. Investments in good professional development can increase the likelihood that teachers will give the program a good try.

School context and individual commitment matter greatly. For example, school-based management is a reform that depends completely upon the understanding, willingness, and skills of teachers, principals, and parents to implement the reform in each school as policymakers intended. Rather than simply *adopting* a reform, studies have established clearly and unequivocally that both teachers and principals *adapt* policies continuously to fit their schools and classrooms.[4]

Policymakers can acknowledge these lessons from the past and understand what it will take to implement reforms as intended. Educators can help identify what is needed to make reforms work. The result should be policies that provide an appropriate mix of incentives, guidance, and help that leaves room for differences from one place to the next and one person to the next.

One size cannot fit all. One trap that snares all kinds of reforms is that no single solution—one curriculum, one kind of instruction, one particular program—will fit all students and teachers everywhere. What appeals to policymakers looking for efficiencies is that a uniform program appears easier to administer and control—and is often less expensive—than tailoring programs

to diverse contexts.

It should be no surprise that many differences exist among states, districts, schools, teachers, and students, given the nation's 50 states and nearly 15,000 school districts with almost 90,000 public schools and more than 3 million teachers instructing almost 50 million students. From differences in neighborhood wealth and community culture to variations in student backgrounds and teacher knowledge, these differences in local context have a huge impact on whether a reform is embraced, how it is carried out, and whether it succeeds. What works well in one school or district is not guaranteed to work in another.

Teachers and principals repeatedly explain that what really matters are the particular children they have in their schools and classrooms. Researchers who have studied reforms know that the particular skills, knowledge, and beliefs of teachers and their bosses also matter in whether and how a reform is put into practice. So, for example, a policy that mandates a highly structured reading program or K-8 organization may fit some settings but not others. To succeed, policies must be adaptable and flexible.

Reject extremes. Education reform has long been characterized as a pendulum incapable of stopping in the middle. For decades, debates over teaching reading (phonics vs. whole-language), math (computation vs. concepts) and writing (grammar vs. content) have polarized policymakers, practitioners, and parents. It may come as a surprise, then, to learn that these "wars" are fought largely with words in speeches, articles, and conferences, not in actual classroom practices. More often than not, research shows, teachers reject extremist positions and find the best solution to be a balance between polar opposites.[5]

Similarly, extreme positions are staked out around "scripted curriculum" and "teacher-invented curriculum." At one extreme, advocates assume that teachers are unable to exercise any judgment and therefore need textbooks that specify word-for-word what they should say to their students. At the other extreme, teachers are viewed as creative inventors, who can design their own curricula, with minimal tools and materials. Most educators reject both extremes, yet they find little support for the middle ground from textbook publishers and district leaders.

Policies that insist on extreme positions invite resistance. To increase the likelihood that programs will lead to desired results, policymakers and the public must seek a middle ground. One such option is to provide choices in reading programs, for example, or provide flexibility to educators to adapt approaches to their circumstances.

Déjà vu all over again. No wonder the distilled wisdom that teachers and principals offer newcomers to school reform is: "Stay in one place long enough and the same reform returns like a bad penny." Time and again, policies that promote curricular change or rely on tests to determine students' futures have been tried, yet few policymakers ever looked in the rearview mirror for help in shaping policies. Only with evidence about why policies did or did not work out as intended will reformers be spared predictable failures. Evaluations of earlier reforms don't provide ready answers to today's questions, but they do provide considerable guidance on what it takes to increase a reform's likelihood of success. Policymakers and citizens can ask more questions about what happened when similar reforms were tried in the past.

Don't throw out the baby with the bathwater. Policies can at best be only hunches about what will work in schools, and even the best guesses, grounded in all available evidence, are no guarantee of success. Policymakers and citizens need to keep an eye on what happens to reforms and an ear out for the reactions of teachers and students. Negative reactions and problems are not necessarily signs that a reform should be abandoned, but they likely point to needed adjustments. Figuring out the right adjustments may require more systematic information gathering. Neither abandoning a reform prematurely nor steadfastly sticking with something that isn't working even if it is politically popular will contribute to improving schools.

Treating reform policies as ideas to be improved upon—or rejected—is a sensible (and morally responsible) way of dealing with policies that have important consequences for both adults and children.

Are the conditions for success in place?

School reforms contain assumptions about what teachers and students already know how to do and what it will take for them to carry out the reforms, but are they accurate? Whether administrators and teachers change what they do to conform to a new reform policy depends on a host of factors, many beyond the control of policymakers. But one factor is under their control: providing the resources to ensure that educators understand and know how to do what they are being asked to do.

Ready or not. Policymakers are typically too far removed from the classroom to fully appreciate what teachers and principals need to have in place to make reforms work. In the absence of discussions with educators, school reform policies are likely to ignore the minimal conditions and resources needed for a reform to have a chance of success. For example, many reforms assume that teachers and administrators have what they need to do a better job, including not only the know-how, but also the necessary materials, help, and professional development. In fact, the conditions present in the poorest and lowest-performing schools are often the opposite of what is needed for improvement. Without dealing directly with issues of distrust and racism, as well as poor training and other needs, efforts to change instruction will fall flat.

Citizens must call attention to the real conditions for teaching and learning in their schools and ensure that policymakers hear directly from educators.

No cheap fix. Too many reforms are promoted as if school improvement aimed at higher academic achievement can be done on the cheap. Creating the conditions for success requires far more than grabbing at innovations. For example, as we have shown, reforms cannot succeed without well-trained teachers. This will mean hiring tens of thousands of such teachers and providing training to those already in the classroom. If the professional development is of a high caliber, it will require an investment of teachers' time and will likely include coaching or mentoring as teachers learn a new approach. So the costs for additional highly skilled people must be included.

Yet policymakers predictably choose to spend millions of dollars on new tests that every child must take rather than the billions it would cost to raise teacher salaries, to attract and keep qualified teachers, and to retrain current teachers. This happens even though a 2005 Educational Testing Service public opinion poll showed that 80 percent of Americans agree that teacher salaries should be increased even if it means raising taxes.[6]

This quest for cheap fixes becomes especially evident in the persistent failure of low-income, largely minority urban schools and many rural schools. So many reforms presume that schools alone are responsible for catastrophic dropout rates, unyielding achievement gaps, and high turnover among school leaders and staffs. Thus, policymakers act as though standards-based curriculum, testing, and accountability measures will remedy these severe problems while failing to provide the resources teachers need and the support necessary beyond the schools, from health services to housing. Insufficient resources will doom the best of reform ideas. Although money is no guarantee of success, lack of money predictably leads to failure.

Additional costs arise from the unexpected consequences of reform policies. Under California's class-size-reduction policy, for example, two major costs went unanticipated.

One: the dollar cost for additional classroom space for every school in the state. The other: the cost of lower teacher quality in the state's poorest schools. Reducing class size in kindergarten through 3rd grade meant that every elementary school needed to hire new teachers right away. This resulted in hiring tens of thousands of uncertified teachers, most of whom ended up teaching in the poorest schools.[7]

Other costs are quite predictable. Unlike prescription drugs, however, the possible negative side effects of reform policies are rarely mentioned, meaning they cannot be weighed against possible benefits. For example, holding 3rd graders back based on one test score could contribute to future failure and dropout rates. Similarly, denying diplomas to students who fail to pass a graduation test means that some students, mostly minority, will leave school without the credential considered essential for even an entry-level job.

Policymakers and citizens alike need to be aware of the real costs of underwriting major reform efforts. If the necessary money is not forthcoming, policymakers and the public should adjust their expectations accordingly. It makes no sense to assume that lofty goals can be achieved regardless of whether the needed resources are in place.

An Ounce of Prevention. Waiting until students reach kindergarten to begin to "close the achievement gap" makes both the challenge and the costs extraordinary. For school reforms to succeed, reforms directed to gaps in learning at a much earlier age are essential. In fact, prenatal care is the starting point for many later learning problems. It is indisputable that gaps in achievement are closely related to income—poor children start school significantly behind their more affluent peers. Attention to gaps, most of which can be traced to poverty, means attention to known problems before children reach school age.

Although such investments would be enormously expensive, continued inattention is even more expensive. High dropout rates for poor and minority students exact huge costs on society. Those who drop out are far more likely to end up unemployed and in jail, both of which cost society considerably more than public schooling.[8] If the goals of school reform are to be realized, it's going to mean reaching beyond the bounds of school reform policies.

These guidelines may help readers make sense of school reforms, to cut through the hype to see both the promise and the pitfalls. Simple answers and hoped-for miracles don't make a dent in the real world of schools and classrooms, except to fan disillusionment. We believe we have posed questions worth asking of any reform and offered lessons about the journey from policy to practice.

The good ideas underlying the reforms reviewed here, and many others not included, deserve nurturing. Yet, it's important to remember that the benefits of change can easily get lost in the translation from good ideas into policies and from policies into classroom practice.

Reformers and policymakers of all stripes must try to understand what motivates and helps teachers and students to do more and what does not, especially in the nation's most challenging classrooms. The more they understand, the more likely it is that their ideas and the policies based on those ideas will reach the target and show results.

If policymakers and citizens adjust their expectations for reform to reflect the investments, their disappointments will diminish. If those who champion good ideas keep their eyes on the classroom, they can keep school reforms on track.

Endnotes

NOTE: All Web data cited below were retrieved between March 1, 2005, and Aug. 30, 2005.

SECTION ONE

1 www.achieve.org/achieve.nsf/
1999Summit_Speeches-
Gerstner?OpenForm

2 According to the Association of American Publishers, elementary and secondary standardized test sales grew by more than 12 percent from 2003 to 2004 to nearly $924 million. www.publishers.org/industry/index.cfm In 2002, the PBS series, "Frontline," reported that test sales were $7 million in 1955, $263 million in 1997. www.pbs.org/wgbh/pages/frontline/shows/schools/testing/companies.html

3 National Center on Education Statistics, National Assessment of Educational Progress, "The Nation's Report Card. 2004 Long-Term Trends. Reading and Mathematics Assessments. National Trends in Reading and Mathematics by Average Scale Scores."

4 Lynn Olson, "A Proficient Score Depends on Geography," Education Week, Feb. 2, 2002; pp. 1, 14-15.

5 Pat Kossan, Anne Ryman, and Ryan Konig; "More Kids Pass '05 AIMS," The Arizona Republic, July 13, 2005. www.azcentral.com/families/education/articles/0713aims13.html

6 Marguerite Roza and Paul T. Hill, "How Within-District Spending Inequities Help Some Schools Fail" and Kati Haycock, "The Elephant in the Living Room," in Brookings Papers on Education Policy: 2004 Diane Ravitch, ed. Brookings Institution Press, 2004.

7 Press Release: News from the Committee on Education and the Workforce, Rep. John Boehner, Chairman, Feb. 11, 2003.

8 W. James Popham, "Why Standardized Tests Don't Measure Educational Quality," Educational Leadership, March 1999, pp. 8-14.

9 Erik W. Robelen, "State Reports on Progress Vary Widely," Education Week, Sept. 3, 2003; pp. 1, 37.

10 Dan Hardy, "Rule changes aided school progress," Philadelphia Inquirer, Oct. 28, 2004.

11 In late 2005, the U.S. Department of Education announced waivers allowing a few states to measure progress instead of simply reporting whether the standard was reached.

12 Henry Braun, "Reconsidering the Impact of High-Stakes Testing," RR-03-29 ETS 2003.

13 Brian M. Stecher, Tammi Chun, Sheila Barron, and Karen Ross; "The Effects of the Washington State Education Reform on Schools and Classrooms: Initial Findings," RAND Corp., Santa Monica, Calif.; 2000.

14 Lorraine M. McDonnell and Craig Choisser, "Testing and Teaching: Local Implementation of New State Assessments," CSE Technical Report 442, September 1997. National Center for Research on Evaluation, Standards, and Student Testing (CRESST) UCLA; Dan Koretz, Karen Mitchell, Sheila Barron, and Sarah Keith, "Final Report: Perceived Effects of the Maryland School Performance Assessment Program," CSE Technical Report 409, March 1996.

15 Joshua Benton and Holly K. Hacker, "Poor schools' TAKS surges raise cheating questions," Dallas Morning News, Dec. 30, 2004. www.dallasnews.com/sharedcontent/dws/dn/education/stories/121904dnmetcheating.64fa3.html

16 Lawrence A. Uzzell, "No Child Left Behind: The Dangers of Centralized Education Policy," Policy Analysis, No. 544, The Cato Institute, May 31, 2005; p. 15.

17 Heinrich Mintrop and Tina Trujillo, "Corrective Action in Low-Performing Schools: Lessons for NCLB Implementation from State and District Strategies in First-Generation Accountability Systems," CSE Report 641. National Center for Research on Evaluation, Standards, and Student Testing, UCLA, December 2004.

18 Carmen DeNavas-Walt, Bernadette D. Proctor, and Robert J. Mills; "Income, Poverty, and Health Insurance Coverage in the United States: 2003. Current Population Reports," U. S. Census Bureau, August 2004.

19 Kati Haycock and Karin Chenoweth, "Choosing to make a difference," American School Board Journal, April 2005, p. 28.

20 NAEP Long-Term Trends. http://nces.ed.gov/nationsreportcard/ltt/results2004/sub-reading-race.asp

21 On closer inspection, some researchers have suggested that narrowing of the racial gaps in Texas was more illusory than real—the result of a limit on how high the top students could score and high dropout rates. National data from 1992 to 1998 suggest an increasing gap during much of the 1990s in Texas and the country overall, "NAEP The Nation's Report Card Reading Highlights 2003," http://nces.ed.gov/nationsreportcard/reading/results2003/stateracegap-g4.asp

22 Lynn Olson, "A 'Proficient' Score Depends on Geography," Education Week, Feb. 20, 2002; pp. 1, 14-15.

23 David J. Hoff, "Texas Judge Rules Funds Not Enough," Education Week, Sept. 22, 2004; pp. 1, 30.

24 Few incentives exist to develop better curricula. A handful of publishing houses produce most of the tests and textbooks, and their incentive is to maximize sales across states, which leads to an emphasis on breadth and catering to the demands of the large states with statewide textbook adoption policies. See Chester E. Finn and Diane Ravitch, "The Mad, Mad World of Textbook Adoption," Fordham Institute, 2004.

25 "Closing the Achievement Gap" issue brief, National Governors Association, May 27, 2003.

26 Sam Dillon, "Charter Schools Alter Map of Public Education in Dayton," New York

Times, March 27, 2005; p. 15

27 Keisha Hegamin, "Real Choice Should Be Available for All," *Philadelphia Public School Notebook,* Fall 2003. www.thenotebook.org/editions/2003/fall/real.htm

28 Timothy Egan, "Failures Raise Questions for Charter Schools," *New York Times,* April 5, 2002; p. A14.

29 *Pierce* v. *Society of Sisters* (1925). Available online at: http://straylight.law.cornell.edu/supct/html/historics/USSC_CR_0268_0510_ZO.html

30 For data on charter schools, see Center for Education Reform Web site, www.edreform.com

31 U.S. Government Accountability Office, "School Vouchers: Characteristics of Privately Funded Programs," GAO-02-752, September 2002.

32 See U.S. Department of Education Web site devoted to No Child Left Behind Act of 2001. www.ed.gov/nclb/landing.jhtml?src=pb

33 Milton Friedman, "The Role of Government in Education," in R. Solo (Ed.), *Economics and the Public Interest* (New Brunswick, N.J.: Rutgers University Press, 1955); John Chubb and Terry Moe, *Politics, Markets, and America's Schools* (Washington, D.C.: Brookings Institution Press, 1990); For a synthesis and scathing analysis of the research in various disciplines' appraisal of choice both public and private, see Joseph Viteritto, "Schoolyard Revolutions: How Research on Urban School Reform Undermines Reform," *Political Science Quarterly,* 118 (2), 2003, pp. 233-257.

34 Michael Casserly, "Driving Change," *Education Next,* 2004. www.educationnext.org/20043/32.html

35 Jennifer Mrozowski, "Charters have high turnover," *The Enquirer,* July 3, 2005.

36 Dan Goldhaber, "School Choice: An Examination of the Empirical Evidence on Achievement, Parental Decision Making, and Equity," *Educational Researcher,* 28(9), 1999, pp. 16-25; Katrina Bulkley and Jennifer Fisler, "A Decade of Charter Schools: From Theory to Practice," CPRE

Policy Briefs, RB-35, April 2002. Diana Schemo, "Nation's Charter Schools Lagging Behind, U.S. Test Scores Reveal," *New York Times,* Aug. 17, 2004; p. A21; Michael Dobbs, "Charter Students Fare No Better, Study Says," *Washington Post,* Dec. 16, 2004; p. A3; Frederick M. Hess, *Revolution at the Margins* (Washington, D.C.: Brookings Institution Press, 2002).

37 Frederick M. Hess, *Revolution at the Margins* (Washington, D.C.: Brookings Institution Press, 2002); Christopher Lubienski, "Innovation in Education Markets: Theory and Evidence on the Impact of Competition and Choice in Charter Schools," *American Educational Research Journal,* 40(2), 2003, pp. 395-443. Bulkley and Fisler, "A Decade of Charter Schools: From Theory to Practice."

38 Monte Whaley, "Owens Signs School Voucher Bill," *Denver Post,* April 17, 2003. Evidence about more competition among schools leading to improvement at no higher cost comes from New Zealand, a country with a national system of education where local school trustees run individual schools (as of 1990) and parents can choose any school they wish (as of 1991). Two researchers have explored this national experiment and found mixed results; that is, general satisfaction among parents with the reform, migrating of social classes to various schools, teacher dissatisfaction, and deep concern among national policymakers over poor-performing schools. To what degree researchers and policymakers can apply the New Zealand experience to the United States is unclear, but the decade-long experiment suggests caution, at the minimum. See Edward Fiske and Helen Ladd, *When Schools Compete: A Cautionary Tale* (Washington, D.C.: The Brookings Institution, 2000); Helen Ladd and Edward Fiske, "Does Competition Improve Teaching and Learning? Evidence from New Zealand," *Educational Evaluation and Policy Analysis,*" 25(1), 1003: pp. 97-112.

39 "Trends in Private School Enrollments," U.S. Department of Education, National Center for Education Statistics. Available online at: http://nces.ed.gov/programs/coe/2005/section1/table.asp?tableID=225

40 U.S. Department of Education, National Center for Education Statistics, "Issue Brief: 1.1 Million Homeschooled Students in the United States in 2003," July 2004, p. 1.

41 Roger Lowenstein, "The Quality Cure?" *New York Times Magazine,* March 13, 2005; p. 50.

42 Carolyn Kelley, "Making Merit Pay Work" www.asbj.com/schoolspending/kelley.html

43 Richard Murnane and David Cohen, "Merit Pay and the Evaluation Problem: Why Most Merit Pay Plans Fail and a Few Survive," *Harvard Educational Review,* 56(1), 1986, p. 15.

44 www.achieve.org/achieve.nsf/1999Summit_ActionStatement?OpenForm

45 Diana Schemo, "When Students' Gains Help Teachers' Bottom Line," *New York Times,* May 9, 2004; p. 15.

46 Kerby Meyers, "Performance Anxiety," *Education Week,* Nov. 1, 2004; Public Agenda, "America's Teachers: Don't Make Us Scapegoats," poll of teachers, www.publicagenda.org. "Statement by Mayor Michael Bloomberg on the Panel's Recommendation in the campaign for Fiscal Equity," Nov. 30, 2004. No Child Left Behind, Title II, Part A www.ed.gov/nclb/overview/intro/progsum/sum_pg6.html

47 Excerpts of Gov. Arnold Schwarzenegger's State of the State Address, Jan. 6, 2005. www.signonsandiego.com/uniontrib/20050106/news_lz1n6excerpts.html

48 Brendan Rapple, "Payment by Results: An Example of Assessment in Elementary Education in 19th Century Britain," *Education Policy Analysis Archives,* 2(1), 1994. http://epaa.asu.edu/epaa/v2n1.html

49 The Teaching Commission, "Teaching at Risk: A Call to Action," January 2004, p. 24.

50 Ibid.

51 Debra Viadero, "Big City Mayors' Control of Schools Yields Mixed Results," *Education Week,* Sept. 11, 2000; p. 8; Geeta Anand, "Menino Pledges Better Schools," *Boston Globe,* Jan. 18, 1996; p. 1.

52 Michael Usdan, "Boston: The Stars Finally in Alignment," in L.Cuban and M. Usdan (eds.), *Powerful Reforms with Shallow Roots* (New York: Teachers College Press, 2003), pp. 38-53.

53 Michael Kirst, "Mayoral Influence, New Regimes, and Public School Governance," CPRE Research Report, RR-049, May 2002 (Philadelphia: Consortium for Policy Research in Education, University of Pennsylvania, Graduate School of Education). For Detroit, see Christine MacDonald and Brad Heath, "Detroit School Reform Falters," *Detroit News*. Oct. 24, 2004. www.detnews.com/2004/specialreport/0410/24/a01-312953.htm

54 Elissa Gootman and David Herszenhorn, "Mayor Hails 'New Era' in Schools Amid Crowding Fears," *New York Times*, Sept.5, 2003; p. B4.

55 Karla Scoon Reid, "Mayors Stepping Up To Improve Quality of City Schools," *Education Week*, April 9, 2003; p. 8.

56 For example, Chicago school councils consist of six parents, two community members, two teachers, and the principal. In Kentucky, school councils are composed of the principal, three teachers, and two parents.

57 Tracy Dell'Angela, "85 schools get reward of freedom: City's top performers cleared to teach and spend as they see fit," *Chicago Tribune* online edition, June 6, 2005.

58 David Tyack, "School Governance in the United States: Historical Puzzles and Anomalies" in *Decentralization and School Improvement*, Jane Hannaway and Martin Carnoy, eds. (San Francisco: Jossey-Bass Publishers)

59 Ibid.

60 William G. Ouchi, "Making Schools Work," *Education Week*, Sept. 3, 2003; pp. 44, 56.

61 Angus McBeath quoted in "An Edmonton Journey" by Jeff Archer, *Education Week*, Jan. 26, 2005; pp. 33-36.

62 Patrick Ryan, "Can't Let Go," *Education Next*, Winter 2001

63 Jeff Archer op cit.

SECTION TWO

1 Ronald Edmonds, "Effective Schools for the Urban Poor," *Educational Leadership*, 37:1, 15-24, September 1979.

2 Thomas J. Peters and Robert H. Waterman Jr., *In Search of Excellence: Lessons from America's Best-Run Companies*. (New York: Harper & Row Publishers, Inc. 1982)

3 Kati Haycock and Karin Chenoweth, "Choosing to make a difference: How schools and districts are beating the odds and narrowing the achievement gap," *American School Board Journal*, April 2005.

4 Charles Handy, "The Handy Guide to the Gurus of Management," Episode 4, BBC English. www.bbc.co.uk/worldservice/learningenglish/work/handy/transcripts/peters.pdf

5 Richard Rothstein, *Class and Schools*. (Washington D.C.: Economic Policy Institute 2004)

6 Melissa Roderick, Mimi Engel, and Jenny Nagaoka; "Ending Social Promotion: Results from Summer Bridge," Consortium on Chicago School Research, February 2003.

7 NCES Dropout Rates in the United States: 1995. NCES 97-473 (http://nces.ed.gov/pubs/dp95/97473-5.asp); National Research Council. "Promotion and Retention" in *High stakes: Testing for tracking, Promotion, and Graduation*. Jay P. Heubert and Robert M. Hauser, editors. National Academy Press Washington, D.C. 1999.

8 Shane E. Jimerson, "A synthesis of grade retention research: Looking backward and moving forward," *The California School Psychologist*, Vol. 6, pp. 47-59, 2001; Jenny Nagaoka and Melissa Roderick, "Ending Social Promotion: The effects of retention," Consortium on Chicago School Research, April 2004.

9 Pete Goldschmidt, "When Can Schools Affect Dropout Behavior? A Longitudinal Multilevel Analysis," *American Education Research Journal*, Winter 1999. Vol. 36 No 4, pp. 715-738.

10 Nagaoka & Roderick op cit.

11 Lorrie S. Shepherd and Mary L. Smith, *Flunking grades: Research and policies on retention*. 1989. (London: Falmer Press).

12 National Research Council, "Promotion and Retention" in *High stakes: Testing for tracking, Promotion, and Graduation*. Jay P. Heubert and Robert M. Hauser, editors. National Academy Press Washington, D.C. 1999. Shane E. Jimerson, "A synthesis of grade retention research: Looking backward and moving forward," *The California School Psychologist*, Vol. 6, pp. 47-59, 2001; Melissa Roderick and Jenny Nagaoka, "Retention Under Chicago's High-Stakes Testing Program: Helpful, Harmful, or Harmless?" *Education Evaluation and Policy Analysis*, Winter 2005, Vol. 27. No. 4, pp. 309-340.

13 Jeffrey Gettleman, "The Segregated Classrooms of a Proudly Diverse School," *New York Times*, April 3, 2005; p.31.

14 James Gallagher, "When Ability Grouping Makes Good Sense," *Education Week*, Oct. 28, 1992. www.edweek.org/ew/articles/1992/10/28/08galla.h12.html; Arguments for and against tracking are summarized in Joseph Kahne, *Reframing Educational Policy* (New York: Teachers College Press, 1996) pp. 59-68; Jeannie Oakes, *Keeping Track* (New Haven, Conn.: Yale University Press, 1985), pp. 15-39.

15 Debra Viadero, "On The Wrong Track," *Teacher Magazine*, January 1999, pp. 22-23.

16 Peter Schmidt, "Debate Over Ability Grouping Gains High Profile," *Education Week*, Oct. 13, 1993. www.edweek.org/ew/articles/1993/10/13/16side.h12.html?

17 Maureen Hallinan, "The Detracking Movement," *Education Next*, Fall 2004. www.educationnext.org/20044/72.html; Jeannie Oakes and Amy Wells, "Detracking for High Student Achievement," *Educational Leadership*, 55, 1998, pp. 38-41.

18 Tom Loveless, "The Tracking and Ability Grouping Debate," Washington, D.C.: Thomas Fordham Foundation, 2003. www.edexcellence.net/foundation/publication/publication.cfm?id=127

19 Bill Gates' prepared remarks to National Governors Association/Achieve Summit Feb. 26, 2005. www.achieve.org/achieve.nsf/2005Summit?OpenForm

20 Achieve 2005 Summit Briefing Book, February 2005, p. 15. www.achieve.org/achieve.nsf/StandardForm3?openform&parentuniid=B277BD2D98CE9CA485256FEF00711757

21 Estimates of dropout and graduation rates are hotly debated. A consensus has emerged around 70 percent as the current estimated graduation rate, but there is less agreement on how much lower the rate is than in the past. See "Counting High School Graduates when Graduates Count: Measuring Graduation Rates under the High Stakes of NCLB," C.B. Swanson and D. Chaplin, February 2003, Urban Institute. www.urban.org/urlprint.cfm?ID=8299 See also Paul Barton, *One-Third of a Nation: Rising Dropout Rates and Declining Opportunities,* Educational Testing Service, February 2005.

22 National Center for Public Policy and Higher Education, Policy Alert: The Educational Pipeline: Big Investment, Big Returns; April 2004, Available at: www.highereducation.org/reports/pipeline/. Note that these estimates vary depending upon definitions of continuing one's education (immediately or within a certain number of years after high school graduation) and the number of years used for defining "on time" graduation from college.

23 J.P Greene and M.A. Winters, "Public High School Graduation and College-Readiness Rates: 1991-2002," Education Working Paper, No. 8, Manhattan Institute for Policy Research, February 2005.

24 P.A. Wasley et al, "Small Schools: Great Strides. A Study of New Small Schools in Chicago," Bank Street College of Education, New York, 2000.

25 Tony Wagner, "The Case for 'New Village' Schools: New Small Schools Foster a Different Kind of Accountability," *Education Week,* Dec. 5, 2001; pp. 42, 56.

26 Erik W. Robelen, "Gates High Schools Get Mixed Review in Study." *Education Week,* Nov. 16, 2005; pp. 1, 20.

27 Sarah Dewees, The School-within-a-School Model, ERIC Clearinghouse on Rural Education and Small Schools, ED43847, 1999, www.ericdigests.org/ 2000-4/school.htm

28 D.R. Lillard and P.P. DeCicca, "Higher standards, more dropouts? Evidence within and across time," *Economics of Education Review 20* (2001), pp. 459-473.

29 Debra Viadero, "Math Emerges as Big Hurdle for Teenagers," *Education Week,* March 23, 2005; pp. 1, 16.

30 Lynn Olson, "Calls for Revamping High Schools Intensify," *Education Week,* Jan. 26, 2005; pp. 1, 18-19.

31 For a discussion of effective programs for retaining students and opportunities for those who have dropped out, see Paul Barton, *One-Third of a Nation: Rising Dropout Rates and Declining Opportunities,* Educational Testing Service, February 2005.

32 Bill Gates' prepared remarks to National Governors Association/Achieve Summit Feb. 26, 2005.

33 United States General Accounting Office, "College Completion: Additional Efforts Could Help Education with Its Completion Goals," May 2003, GAO-03-568.

34 Becky Bartindale, "Fewer students admitted to CSU," *San Jose Mercury News.* April 14, 2005; p. B1.

35 See Edison Web site at www.edisonschools.com/schools/s0.html; on Comer schools, see www.rockfound.org/display.asp?context=1&Collection=1&DocID=471&Preview=0&ARCurrent=1; KIPP school data at www.kipp.org/aboutkipp.cfm?pageid=nav6

36 Ronald Edmonds, Op cit.

37 Pamela Bullard and Barbara Taylor, *Making School Reform Happen* (Boston: Allyn Bacon, 1993.)

38 RAND Corp. Research Brief, "A Decade of Whole-School Reform: The New American Schools Experience," 2002. www.rand.org/publications/RB/RB8019/

39 Debra Viadero, "Memphis Scraps Redesign Models In All Its Schools," *Education Week*, Nov. 7, 2001; p. 1, 19.

40 Charles M. Payne and Miriame Kaba, "So Much Reform, So Little Change: Building-Level Obstacles to Urban School Reform," Unpublished manuscript, February 2001.

41 Ibid.

42 Mark Berends, Susan J. Bodilly, and Sheila Nataraj Kirby, *Facing the Challenges of Whole-School Reform: New American Schools After a Decade* (Santa Monica: RAND, 2002), Chapter 7.

43 Determining average class sizes is tricky because of the number of specialized teachers who may work with only a handful of students, e.g., special education teachers. Typically, a school's average class size is calculated by dividing the number of students by the number of teachers, but most counts include specialized teachers resulting in a number lower than the average number of students in regular classrooms.

44 E. Word, J. Johnston, H.P. Bain, et al, "Student/Teacher Achievement Ratio (STAR): Tennessee's K-3 class size study. Final summary report 1985-1990," Nashville: Tennessee Department of Education, 1990.

45 B.A. Nye, J.B. Zaharias, B.D. Fulton, et al, "The Lasting Benefits Study: A continuing analysis of the effect of small class size in kindergarten through third grade on student achievement test scores in subsequent grade levels. Seventh grade technical report," Nashville: Center of Excellence for Research in Basic Skills, Tennessee State University, 1994.

46 Frederick Mosteller, "The Tennessee Study of Class Size in the Early Grades," *Critical Issues For Children and Youths,* Vol. 5, No. 2; Spring/fall 1995.

47 George W. Bohrnstedt and Brian M. Stecher, editors, "What We Have Learned About Class Size Reduction in California," September 2002, Sacramento, Calif.: California Department of Education.

48 Ivor Pritchard, "Reducing Class Size: What Do We Know?" U. S. Department of Education. March 1999, www.ed.gov/pubs/ReducingClass/title.html

49 E. D. Hirsch Jr., "Classroom Research and Cargo Cults," *Policy Review,* No. 115, October 2002.

50 William Schmidt, Curtis McKnight, Richard Houang, et. al., *Why Schools Matter: A Cross-National Comparison of Curriculum and Learning,* pp. 298-301, 308-309. (San Francisco: Jossey-Bass, 2001)

51 National Education Commission on Time and Learning, Prisoners of Time, May 1994: www.ed.gov/pubs/PrisonersOfTime/PoTSch

ool/intro.html and Scot Lehigh, "The Case for Longer School Days," *Boston Globe,* Jan.19, 2005: www.boston.com/news/globe/editorial_opinion/oped/articles/2005/01/19/the_case_for_longer_school_days/

52 www.kipp.org/schoolsinaction.cfm?pageid=nav1; Jennifer Davis and David Farbman, "Rethinking Time: The Next Frontier of Education Reform," *Education Week,* Dec. 1, 2004; pp. 40, 52.

53 National Association for Year Round Education, "Statistical Summaries of Year-Round Education Programs, 2004-2005." www.nayre.org; On year-round schools, exceptions do occur. In many places where school construction has not kept pace with numbers of children attending school, particularly in urban low-income areas, school administrators switched to year-round education to accommodate larger numbers of students. Year-round schools solve the problem of overcrowded schools.

54 Dirk Johnson, "Many Schools Putting an End to Child's Play," *New York Times*, April 7, 1998.

55 Melissa Roderick, Mimi Engel, and Jenny Nagaoka, "Ending Social Promotion: Results from Summer Bridge," Consortium on Chicago School Research, February 2003.

56 National Education Commission on Time and Learning, "Prisoners of Time," May 1994: www.ed.gov/pubs/PrisonersOfTime/PoTSchool/intro.html Anthony Pellegrini and Catherine Bohn, "The Role of Recess in Children's Cognitive Performance and School Adjustment," *Education Researcher*, 34, January/February 2005, pp. 13-19; An-Me Chung and Eugene Hillsman, "Evaluating After-School Programs," *School Administrator* May 2005 (Web edition). www.aasa.org/publications/sa/2005_05/chung.htm; WestEd, "Improving Student Achievement by Extending School: Is It Just a Matter of Time?" 1998: www.wested.org/online_pubs/timeandlearning/TAL_PV.html

57 Priscilla Pardini, "Revival of the K-8 School,"*AASA School Administrator Web Edition*, March 2002.

58 Ibid, p. 3.

59 David Angus, Jeffrey Mirel, and Maris

Vinovskis; "Historical Development of Age Stratification in Schooling," *Teachers College Record*, 90(2), 1988, pp. 213-236; statistics come from Pardini, p. 4.

60 Pardini, op. cit., p. 4.

61 Larry Cuban, "What Happens to Reforms That Last: The Case of the Junior High School," *American Educational Research Journal*, 29(2), 1992, pp. 227-252.

62 Deborah Viadero, "Report Questions Wisdom of Separate Middle Schools," *Education Week,* March 17, 2004; p. 8.

63 Kimberly Reeves, "Figuring and Reconfiguring Grade Spans," *AASA School Administrator Web Edition*, March 2005.

64 Ibid.

65 Robert Balfanz, Kurt Spiridakis, and Ruth Neild; "Will Converting High-Poverty Middle Schools to K-8 Schools Facilitate Achievement Gains?" (Philadelphia: Philadelphia Education Fund, 2002), Appendix.

SECTION THREE

1 NAEP *The Nation's Report Card: Reading Highlights 2003* NCES 2004-452 USED, IES.

2 National Institute of Child Health and Human Development (2000), "*Report of the National Reading Panel. Teaching children to read: an evidence-based assessment of the scientific research literature on reading and its implications for reading instruction.*" www.nichd.nih.gov/publications/nrp/smallbook.htm. See also: Joann Yatvin, *Minority View* (2000) www.nichd.nih.gov/publications/nrp/minorityView.pdf. Other critiques include Siegfried Engelmann, "The Dalmation and Its Spots," *Education Week,* Jan. 28, 2004; and Richard L. Allington, "Ideology is Still Trumping Evidence," *Phi Delta Kappan,* February 2005, pp. 462-8.

3 Catherine E. Snow, M. Susan Burns, and Peg Griffin, editors, "Preventing Reading Difficulties in Children," National Academy of Sciences, National Research Council, 1998.

4 Stanley Pogrow, " The Missing Element in Reducing the Learning Gap: Eliminating the 'Blank Stare,'" *Teachers College Record*, October 2004.

5 David DeSchryver, "Magic of Potter," *The Doyle Report*, Issue 5.30, July 29, 2005.

6 Deputy chancellor for instruction at the New York City Board of Education quoted in *New York Times,* "Teaching by the Book, No Asides Allowed," by Abby Goodnough, May 23, 2001.

7 National Academy of Sciences, op cit., p. 2.

8 NAEP 2003.

9 NAEP 2003.

10 http://xpress.sfsu.edu/archives/news/003333.html.

11 "Mathematics Performance of Students in Grades 4 and 8," http://nces.ed.gov/programs/coe/2005/section2/indicator10.asp. Although the timelines are the same, the rise in scores did not necessarily result from the math standards and new programs.

12 Debra Viadero, "Math Emerges as Big Hurdle for Teenagers,"*Education Week,* March 23, 2005; pp. 1, 16.

13 www.csmonitor.com/2002/1115/p09s01-coop.html (Retrieved Nov. 22, 2002.)

14 Debra Viadero, "Math Emerges as Big Hurdle for Teenagers," op cit.

15 "Mathematics Equals Opportunity," http://www.ed.gov/pubs/math/part2.html

16 Heather C. Hill, Brian Rowan, Deborah Loewenberg Ball; "Effects of Teachers' Mathematical Knowledge for Teaching on Student Achievement," *American Educational Research Journal*. In press.

17 Larry Cuban, *How Teachers Taught: Constancy and Change in American Classrooms 1880-1990.* (Teachers College Press: New York 1993.)

18 Patricia Clark Kenschaft, "Racial Equity Requires Teaching Elementary School Teachers More Mathematics," Notices of the American Mathematical Society, Volume 52, No. 2, pp. 208-212.

19 Ibid.

20 "English Language Learners: Boosting Educational Achievement." American Educational Research Association, *Research Points*, 2(1), 2004, p. 1. Because Hispanics are the largest group of immigrants, much of the chapter focuses on them.

21 *The Condition of Education 2003*, National Center for Educational Statistics. (Washington, D.C.: U.S. Department of Education, 2003), p. 126.

22 Sam Anaya quoted in Mary Ann Zehr, "Oklahoma District Picks Path Less Followed for English-Learners," *Education Week*, May 4, 2005; pp. 20-21.

23 German immigrant boy cited in Kenji Hakuta, *Mirror of Language*, p. 207. (New York: Basic Books, 1986.)

24 David Tyack, *The One Best System*, pp. 106-109. (Cambridge, Mass.: Harvard University Press, 1974.)

25 Ibid.

26 Noel Epstein; *Language, Ethnicity, and the Schools*, pp. 1-3. (Washington, D.C.: Institute for Educational Leadership, 1977.)

27 Michelle Adam, "The Changing Face of ELL Literacy Practices Under No Child Left Behind," *ELL Outlook*, November/December 2004, www.coursecrafters.com/ELL-Outlook/2004/nov_dec/OutLook_NovDec.html

28 NAEP. The Nation's Report Card. Reading. 2003. http://nces.ed.gov/nationsreportcard/reading/results2003/scale-ethnic-compare.asp

29 James Crawford, "English Only Vs. English Only: A Tale of Two Initiatives," http://ourworld.compuserve.com/homepages/JWCRAWFORD/203-227.htm

30 Vickie Lake and Eleni Pappamihiel, "Effective Practices and Principles to Support English Language Learners in Early Childhood Classrooms," *Childhood Education*, 17(2), 2003, pp. 200-203; Wayne Thomas and Virginia Collier, "A National Study of School Effectiveness for Language Minority Students' Long-Term Academic Achievement." Center for Research on Education, Diversity, and Excellence, 2002); Kris Gutierrez et. Al, "Sounding American: The Consequences of New Reforms on English Language Learners," *Reading Research Quarterly*, 37(3), 2002; pp. 328-345.

31 Guadalupe Valdes, *Con Respeto: Bridging the Distance Between Culturally Diverse Families and Schools*. (New York: Teachers College Press, 1996.)

32 Jane L. David, Pamelia Coe, and Patricia J. Kannapel, "Content-Focused Professional Development in Kentucky: A Study of the Middle-School Summer Academies," Partnership for Kentucky Schools, Lexington, Ky; August 2003.

33 Sam Dillon, "'Soccer Mom' Education Chief Plays Hardball," *New York Times*, April 28, 2005.

34 R.F. Elmore and D. Burney (1999), "Investing in teacher learning: Staff development and instructional improvement," in L. Darling-Hammond and G. Sykes (Eds.), *Teaching as the learning profession: Handbook of policy and practice*. (San Francisco: Jossey-Bass Publishers.)

35 Harold W. Stevenson and James W. Stigler, *The Learning Gap*. (New York: Summit Books 1992.)

36 See brief synthesis in G.W. McDiarmid, "Still Missing After All These Years: Understanding the Paucity of Subject-Matter Professional Development in Kentucky," Lexington Ky.: Partnership for Kentucky Schools, April 1999.

37 Mary Kennedy, "Form and Substance in Inservice Teacher Education," Research Monograph, National Institute of Science Education, April 1998.

38 Milbrey W. McLaughlin and Joan E. Talbert (In Press), *Developing Teacher Learning Communities in Schools: A Local Agenda to Improve Student Achievement*. (New York: Teachers College Press.)

39 Judith Warren Little, "Inside Teacher Community: Representations of Classroom Practice," *Teachers College Record*. Volume 105, Number 6, August 2003, pp. 913–945.

40 Harold W. Stevenson and James W. Stigler, *The Learning Gap: Why Our Schools Are Failing and What We Can Learn from Japanese and Chinese Education*. (New York: Summit Books, 1992.)

41 "Technology in Public Schools, 1991-1992: Extract," pp. 1-2. Denver: Quality Education Data, 1992.

42 National Center for Education Statistics Internet Access in U.S. Public Schools and Classrooms: 1994-2003.

43 Chris Kenning, "Student faults schools on computer use," *The Courier-Journal*, July 12, 2005.

44 Holly M. Hart, Elaine Allensworth, Douglas L. Lauen, and Robert M. Gladden; Educational Technology: Availability and Use in Chicago's Public Schools, September 2002, Consortium on Chicago School Research.

45 Henry J. Becker, "Who's wired and who's not: Children's access to and use of computer technology," *The Future of Children*. 10(2). (2000); Barbara Means, William R. Penuel, and Christine Padilla; *The Connected School: Technology and Learning in High School*. 2001.

46 Associated Press, "Test Seeks To Measure Students' Web IQ," Published in USA Today, July 3, 2005.

WHAT CAN REFORMERS AND TAXPAYERS DO?

1 Richard Elmore quoted in Marjorie Coeyman "Just when you thought you knew the rules . . ." *Christian Science Monitor*; July 9, 2002. www.csmonitor.com/2002/0709/p11s01-lepr.html

2 www.naceweb.org/press/display.asp?year=2005&prid=207 (From Job Outlook 2005 National Associate of Colleges and Employers.)

3 Richard B. Anderson, Robert G. St. Pierre, Elizabeth C. Proper, and Linda B. Stebbins, "Pardon us, but what was the question again?: A response to the critique of the Follow Through evaluation," *Harvard Educational Review*, Vol. 48, no. 2, May 1978, pp. 161-170.

4 Milbrey W. McLaughlin, "The Rand Change Agent Study Revisited: Macro Perspectives and Micro Realities," *Educational Researcher*, December 1990, pp. 11-16.

5 See, for example, Larry Cuban, "How Teachers Taught," and Cynthia Coburn, "Collective Sensemaking About Reading; How Teachers Mediate Reading Policy in Their Professional Communities," *Educational Evaluation and Policy Analysis*, 23(2), pp. 145-170.

6 Educational Testing Service, "Public Opinion Poll," June 22, 2005. www.cpwire.com/ archive/2005/6/22/1856.asp

7 Patrick M. Shields, Camille E. Esch, Daniel C. Humphrey, Marjorie E. Wechsler, Christopher M. Chang-Ross, Alix H. Gallagher, Roneeta Guha, Juliet D. Tiffany-Morales, and Katrina R. Woodworth, *The status of the teaching profession 2003.* (Santa Cruz, Calif.: The Center for the Future of Teaching and Learning.)

8 See, for example, www.tc.edu/centers/ EquityCampaign/symposium/resource Details.asp?PresId=6, a series of papers presented at the fall 2005 symposium on "Social Costs of Inadequate Education," Teachers College, Columbia University.

PHOTOGRAPHY INDEX

PAGE 5: Table of Contents
First graders at Public School 33 in New York City. Photo by Todd Plitt

PAGE 14:
A 3rd grader at London Towne Elementary School in Centreville, Va., takes the Benchmark Assessment and Reporting Tool (BART) test. Photo by Christopher Powers

PAGE 48:
A class at Abraham Lincoln High School in Council Bluffs, Iowa. File Photo by Benjamin Tice Smith

PAGE 66:
James P. Comer at the Columbus School in New Haven, Conn. Photo by Terry Dagradi/Yale Medicine Publications

PAGE 80:
A 1st grade teacher reads to her class at Public School 33 in New York City. Photo by Todd Plitt

PAGE 87:
Sixth and 7th graders work on math equations at Kennedy Middle School in El Centro, Calif. Photo by Sandy Huffaker

PAGE 93:
A student at Kennedy Middle School in El Centro, Calif., tackles math problems. Ninety-nine percent of the student body at Kennedy is Hispanic, and some 70 percent speak Spanish as their primary language. Photo by Sandy Huffaker

Index

ABOUT THE AUTHORS

JANE L. DAVID received a doctorate in education and social policy from Harvard University in 1974 after teaching high school mathematics in Washington, D.C.. Since then, her career in research and evaluation has focused on the connections between education policy and how schools and districts improve, particularly those serving children at risk of failure.

Dr. David directs the Bay Area Research Group, a small consulting firm, whose clients range from think tanks and government agencies to foundations and nonprofit organizations. She also conducts strategic reviews for nonprofit organizations and foundations. She has authored more than 100 reports, book chapters, articles, and commissioned papers.

LARRY CUBAN is Professor Emeritus of Education at Stanford University. He has taught courses in the methods of teaching social studies, the history of school reform, curriculum, and instruction, and leadership. He has been faculty sponsor of the Stanford/Schools Collaborative and Stanford's Teacher Education Program.

Trained as a historian, Dr. Cuban received a B.A. from the University of Pittsburgh in 1955 and an M.A. from Cleveland's Case-Western Reserve University three years later. He subsequently taught high school social studies in low-income schools for 14 years and directed a teacher education program that prepared returning Peace Corps volunteers to teach in inner-city schools. On completing his Ph.D. work at Stanford University in 1974, he assumed the superintendency of the Arlington, Va., Public Schools, a position he held until returning to Stanford in 1981. Since 1988, he has taught semester-long classes three times in local high schools. Between 1981 and 2001, students in the School of Education selected him for an award in excellence in teaching seven times.

His major research interests focus on the history of curriculum and instruction, educational leadership, school reform and the uses of technology in classrooms. His most recent books are: *The Blackboard and the Bottom Line: Why Schools Can't Be Businesses (2004)*; *Powerful Reforms with*

Shallow Roots: Improving Urban Schools 2003 (edited with Michael Usdan); *Why Is It So Hard To Get Good Schools?* (2003); *Oversold and Underused: Computers in the Classroom* (2001); *How Can I Fix It? An Educators' Guide to Solving Problems and Managing Dilemmas (2001)*; *Reconstructing the Common Good in Education: Managing Intractable American Dilemmas*, 2000 (edited with Dorothy Shipps); and *How Scholars Trumped Teachers: Change without Reform in University Curriculum, Teaching, and Research, 1890-1990* (1999).

EDUCATION WEEK PRESS

Education Week Press is one arm of Editorial Projects in Education, an independent, nonprofit corporation dedicated to elevating the level of discourse on American K-12 education and best known as the publisher of *Education Week*. For 25 years, *Education Week* has kept educators, policymakers, and others abreast of important developments in schools. EPE also publishes *Teacher Magazine* and two highly regarded annual reports, *Quality Counts* and *Technology Counts*. EPE's Web site, edweek.org, is an award-winning source of up-to-the-minute news, information, and resources for educators, as well as in-depth research on issues preK-12. **www.edweek.org**

NOTES

NOTES

NOTES

NOTES

Need Another Copy? Order It Now!

Title	Price	Quantity	Item Total
Cutting Through The Hype	$19.95		

Name

Title

School/Organization

Address

City   State   Zip

Phone

E-mail

☐ VISA/MC/AMEX#   Exp Date

Signature

☐ Check enclosed. (Make payable to Education Week Press)

Mail Coupon to:
EDUCATION WEEK PRESS
P.O. Box 554
Mt. Morris, IL 61054

For faster service:
Toll-Free: 800-788-5692
Fax: 815-734-5864
Online: http://edweek.k-online.biz

Need Another Copy? Order It Now!

Title	Price	Quantity	Item Total
Cutting Through The Hype	$19.95		

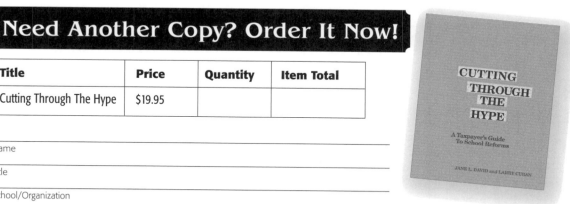

Name

Title

School/Organization

Address

City   State   Zip

Phone

E-mail

☐ VISA/MC/AMEX#   Exp Date

Signature

☐ Check enclosed. (Make payable to Education Week Press)

Mail Coupon to:
EDUCATION WEEK PRESS
P.O. Box 554
Mt. Morris, IL 61054

For faster service:
Toll-Free: 800-788-5692
Fax: 815-734-5864
Online: http://edweek.k-online.biz

EDUCATION WEEK®

Stay A Step Ahead

Yes! Please enter my one-year subscription to EDUCATION WEEK. I will save almost 40% off the cover price and enjoy full access to edweek.org.

■ Bill me. ■ Payment enclosed.

44 print issues and premium online content for only

$79⁹⁴

Name _____ Title _____

School/Organization _____

Address _____

City _____ State _____ Zip _____

E-mail _____

B6TAX1

Mail or fax coupon to: EDUCATION WEEK • P.O. Box 2083 • Marion, OH 43306 • Fax: 740-389-5574
For faster service: Phone: 800-728-2790 • Online: http://www.edweek.org/offer2.html

---

EDUCATION WEEK®

Stay A Step Ahead

Yes! Please enter my one-year subscription to EDUCATION WEEK. I will save almost 40% off the cover price and enjoy full access to edweek.org.

■ Bill me. ■ Payment enclosed.

44 print issues and premium online content for only

$79⁹⁴

Name _____ Title _____

School/Organization _____

Address _____

City _____ State _____ Zip _____

E-mail _____

B6TAX2

Mail or fax coupon to: EDUCATION WEEK • P.O. Box 2083 • Marion, OH 43306 • Fax: 740-389-5574
For faster service: Phone: 800-728-2790 • Online: http://www.edweek.org/offer2.html